SONQ DYNASTY MUSICAL SOURCES
AND THEIR INTERPRETATION

HARVARD-YENCHING INSTITUTE
Monograph Series • Volume 16

SONQ DYNASTY
MUSICAL SOURCES

and Their

INTERPRETATION

by Rulan Chao Pian

HARVARD UNIVERSITY PRESS

Cambridge, Massachusetts

To My Parents

Preface

Only two musical works dated before the Sonq dynasty (A.D. 960–1279) are known to be extant today: one is *Iou Lan* 幽蘭, a piece for the *chyn,* the seven-stringed zither, in a Tarng manuscript, ascribed to a certain Chiou Ming 丘明 of the sixth century; the other is a set of twenty-five melodies for the four-stringed lute, *pyiba,* found in the Duenhwang caves and dated some time before A.D. 933. Both are unique examples of their kind, and their deciphering involves numerous uncertainties. The notation for *Iou Lan* is a prototype of the present-day *chyn* tablature. For the *pyiba* notation there is nothing comparable in other Chinese sources so far discovered, but there are related materials in Japan.

From the Sonq dynasty on we find musical sources more obviously related to Chinese works of later times. Throughout the entire Sonq period various kinds of important musical documents are found. But for more than a century shortly after Sonq, for some unknown reason, no music of any kind survives. It is because of this distribution of available source materials that I have chosen the Sonq dynasty as a unit, not because I attribute to this political period any more basic significance in the history of Chinese music. Politically, the three centuries of the Sonq are isolated by a preceding fifty years of anarchy and a hundred years of subsequent foreign domination, but there is as yet no basis for the periodization of Chinese music.

By and large I have based this survey on primary sources. Source materials of which I have made little use are the musical compilations of Ming and Ching periods that probably contain music of Sonq and earlier date. Such compilations were often done under imperial order, and the compilers presumably had access to old and rare editions preserved in the royal libraries. But the origins of the pieces in these compilations are seldom clearly indicated, and to confirm the dates of these so-called ancient pieces is a task beyond the scope of the present survey. I have relied on only one Ming source for musical examples which are specifically attributed to a known Sonq work.

PREFACE

Besides musical examples, the Sonq dynasty has left us musical treatises, historical records about musical activities, and literary works containing interesting passages on music. They were written both by court officials and by private scholars; some were historians, some poets, and a few were practical musicians.

The reason why we have all this material is partly that wood-block printing was developed in the early years of the Sonq dynasty. Numerous Sonq works are preserved to this day in the original printed editions. Other Sonq works preserved are in the form of facsimiles, manuscript copies, and reprints, and it is owing to the efforts of Ming and Ching scholars—who were distinguished by their rigorous methods of textual criticism and thorough research—that excellent critical editions of Sonq texts are accessible today.

Eighty-seven different musical examples are found in Sonq sources. Over half of these are ceremonial songs, but within this group there are different types: some are melodies of popular origin; some are intellectual exercises so artificial that one doubts whether they were ever really performed as music. There are twenty-seven pieces written in a notation used by Sonq popular musicians. Some appear with lyrics by famous Sonq poets; some seem to be just stock melodies without text. The seven *chyn* melodies, especially the five without text, in a purely instrumental idiom are perhaps the most spontaneous musical compositions of the entire group of existing Sonq music.

The problems involved in transcribing the different systems of notation are various. Music written with pitch names in Chinese characters simply requires a reliable edition. For the *chyn,* the elaborate system of tablature is practically identical with that of today, and the Sonq treatises show that current methods can be used in determining the pitches of the notes. Unfortunately the original rhythm cannot thus be determined, although because the modern *chyn* notation is also unmeasured, a look at modern practices in *chyn* playing can be suggestive.

The third type of notation, very little known after the Sonq period, is the popular notation used by the Sonq practical musicians. It is a set of symbols some of which can vary in pitch according to the particular mode in use. All Sonq compositions have modal labels because they were presumably composed according to a modal prescription. One needs therefore to find a description of modes most applicable to these works. The standard Sonq treatises give incomplete descriptions; it is only in an incidental description in a personal memoir, about one hundred years earlier than the musical examples, that we find a complete account of the modes which describes all the arbitrary omissions and preferences in the scales. With this aid, every symbol in the music can be read without ambiguity. In order to justify on purely musical grounds the choice of the notes in question, I have also included an analysis of the melodies thus transcribed.

The introduction of foreign modes is a major event in Chinese musical history. However, the generally enthusiastic but somewhat vague description of music in Tarng works made it difficult for later scholars to understand exactly what the modes were. We only know that in the course of time these modes underwent very complicated changes. By Sonq times there were more concrete musical examples and exact descriptions which make it possible for us to define clearly, at least for Sonq, what the theories of modes were, and how they were applied to practical music. Nevertheless there remain unanswered questions. For example, there are disagreements in the definition of the basic scale; and the treatises do not mention the fairly regular patterns of secondary cadences and the use of melody types.

The predilection for theory and antiquarian interests, so typical of Sonq, are well reflected in its music. Many of the ceremonial songs are in the style of another age, or are experimental. Modes not in current use are adopted for both ceremonial and entertainment songs. Even writings on music reflect the Sonq temperament. Unlike the cosmopolitan empire of the Tarng, Sonq China was a self-consciously nationalistic country. Central Asian music, introduced into China in the Tarng period, was synthesized with Chinese music by Sonq times, and its theory incorporated into the Chinese scheme of musico-cosmology. Sonq writers went beyond the eulogies of the power and beauty of music that one finds in Tarng poems and stories to write in great detail about such matters as measuring pitches, making musical instruments, tuning strings, and reading musical notation. Such practical matters occupied the attention of many learned scholars, in part because of their potential application to the revival of ancient ceremonial music.

Some of the Sonq writings on music best known to us today were not immediately well received in their own time. The Neo-Confucianists, among whom the musical scholars were to be found, were rivals of the faction in the government identified with Taoism, and were often out of favor with the Sonq emperors. The works of these Neo-Confucian scholars were at times ignored (Chern Yang's *Yueh Shu*) or openly criticized (Tsay Yuandinq's *Liuhleu Shin Shu*). On the other hand, in subsequent years, because of the bias of Confucian historians, many of these works survived and some became almost canonical (Ju Shi's *Yilii Jingjuann Tongjiee*).

As a result, today we know far less than we should like about some Sonq dynasty musical institutions which exerted real power, such as the Dahshenq Fuu established in Huei Tzong's time. Fortunately, there was no lack of private writers producing invaluable records and historical compilations, done with objectivity and in great detail. These have also survived, and some information can be gathered directly or indirectly from their passages on music.

ACKNOWLEDGMENTS

In 1957 I began to write this study as a doctoral dissertation under the direction of Professors John M. Ward and L. S. Yang. It was their criticism and guidance that made it acceptable as a thesis. Professor Ward has continued to provide helpful advice as I have revised the thesis for publication. I owe Professor Yang, or "Yang Gong" as he is addressed with respectful affection by all those who have been under his tutelage, an even more fundamental debt of gratitude. It was he who first persuaded me to undertake the formal study of Chinese music, who taught me what I know of the various disciplines in the Far Eastern field, and who gave me encouragement when I most needed it.

The materials on which the study is based have been assembled from a variety of libraries, and I am indebted to the several individuals who helped me uncover them. During my trip to Japan in 1959 Professor Kishibe Shigeo kindly placed his rich personal library of musical sources at my disposal, and Miss Fukuda Naomi made arrangements for me to microfilm works from many libraries in Japan. Most of the actual work of writing this study was done in Cambridge, where I enjoyed the unexcelled facilities of the Chinese-Japanese Library at Harvard University and where my task was lightened by the unfailing cooperation of its librarian, Dr. A. K. Chiu, who has a special interest in Chinese musical writings.

In the last decade, there have been many Chinese publications on the Songs of Jiang Kwei. Among these, I have made a thorough comparison of my interpretation with that in the special study by Yang Yinnliou, and part of a study by Chiou Chyongsuen. In the past few years,

PREFACE

Laurence Picken has published detailed studies on several aspects of Sonq dynasty music that have spurred me, in more than one way, to finish my book. Since our emphases are not always the same, I think our works on the whole complement each other. If I seem to be making frequent comments on his articles, it is because they will continue for many years to be standard works in this field. Mention should also be made of Walter Kaufmann's book, *Musical Notations of the Orient* (1967), which also touches on many aspects of Sonq dynasty sources. Unfortunately, it is too late to incorporate it in the discussion in the present book.

My work has greatly benefited from the helpful criticisms of Dr. John L. Bishop and Professor James R. Hightower, who read the entire manuscript in final draft. They improved my English, corrected my Chinese, pointed out facts about Chinese literature, and occasionally gave in to some of my arguments. Dr. Glen W. Baxter, who during the early stages of this study advised me on the section dealing with *tsyr*, and provided the English translation of many book and article titles, continued to help me quietly through various stages of preparation. And finally I wish to thank my husband Ted, who patiently waited for the work to be finished.

R. C. P.

Cambridge, Massachusetts
1967

[xi]

Contents

Tables

Illustrations

SONQ DYNASTY MUSICAL SOURCES
AND THEIR INTERPRETATION

Abbreviations Used in Notes

CTTS   *Chyangtsuen Tsorngshu*
HJAS   *Harvard Journal of Asiatic Studies*
SBBY   *Syhbuh Beyyaw*
SBTK   *Syhbuh Tsorngkan*
SLGJ   *Shyhlin Goangjih*
TSJC   *Tsorngshu Jyicherng*
YYTK   *Yuyuan Tsorngke*

Chapter I

THE SOURCES

Theoretical Treatises

From the very founding of the Sonq dynasty in 960, musical theorists at court were much preoccupied with controversies over the nature and regulation of "correct music," music appropriate for court functions. They agreed in general that the "corrupting" influence of foreign music during the Tarng dynasty (618–906) and the political confusion during the Five Dynasties (906–960) had all but destroyed the tradition of the correct type of music in China. But they disagreed very strongly over what it was that had been lost. There were constant arguments as to whether the absolute pitch of the fundamental note *hwang jong* should be one or three semitones lower than it was supposed to have been in the Later Jou (951–960), whether the bells should be in sets of twelve or sixteen, whether octave notes should be used, and so forth. During the Northern Sonq period (960–1127) the standard of measurement for the pitch pipes was changed six times. These changes often involved other readjustments, such as recasting of the bells and addition or elimination of certain instruments. Numerous treatises were written on these reforms, either by imperial order or on individual initiative. The "Yueh Jyh" (Monograph on Music) in the *Sonq Shyy* (History of the Sonq Dynasty),[1] which describes this musical turmoil in detail, cites over a dozen of these treatises and gives a full list of their contents.[2] The few of these which are fortunately still extant I shall discuss in chronological order.

The first work on my list is the *San Lii Twu* 三禮圖 [The Three Rituals Texts Illustrated],[3] written by Nieh Chorngyih 聶崇義 and presented to

---

[1] This work will be discussed in the section on historical and encyclopedic compilations. Hereafter it will be referred to as the *Sonq History* and cited by the four-digit page numbers of the Kaiming Book Company edition.

[2] A list of 111 books on music is given in the "Yihwen Jyh" [Monograph on Bibliography] of *Sonq History,* 4978c–d.

[3] On the three Ritual classics, all compiled in the Hann dynasty (206 B.C.–A.D. 220), see J. R. Hightower, *Topics in Chinese Literature* (Cambridge, Mass., 1953), p. 4.

the emperor in 996.[4] The date of its first printing is unknown. The Ming bibliophile Mau Jinn (1596–1659) had made a facsimile edition of a Sonq printing (of which we have no further evidence beyond Mau's bibliographical information), and there is a Yuan printing done in 1247.[5] The edition available at present is a photolithographic copy of a third edition based on parts of these two editions.[6]

The work consists of twenty short chapters describing the ceremonial caps and robes that should be worn by the emperor and the empress, the architectural plan of the ceremonial halls, ritual equipment such as vessels and flags, and even an ancient game, played with arrows and targets, for entertaining royal guests. It is in this section on entertainment (chapter 5), called "tour-hwu" 投壺 (pitch pot), that we find descriptions of musical instruments, presumably played during the contest, together with drawings of bells, chimes, zithers, flutes, and various types of wooden percussion instruments. In chapter 7 nine kinds of drums and four kinds of bells are mentioned.

In books of this type authority was always considered more important than originality. Nieh asserted that his book was based upon six previous works on the subject, among which were the writings by Jenq Shyuan (A.D. 127–200), the Hann dynasty authority on the Classics. Still, San Lii Twu was criticized for not following the authorities closely enough.[7] Since the work is an attempt at reconstructing the musical practice of the ancient sages, it cannot be considered a true description of Sonq musical practice, although it may contain some Sonq elements. The real importance of the San Lii Twu is that it is one of the earliest known works to contain illustrations of musical instruments. Although the faithfulness of these illustrations to the originals is open to question, the woodcuts do help modern scholars in identifying some of the names of drums and bells found in the unillustrated treatises of later times. One can see the influence of the San Lii Twu by the frequent quotations made from it, even as late as 1725, in the music section of the Chinese encyclopedia Guujin Twushu Jyicherng.[8]

[4] Date of the colophon by the minister Lii Jyh 李至.

[5] Full title: Shicherng Jenq Shyh Jiashwu Chorngjiaw San Lii Twu 析城鄭氏家塾重校 三禮圖 [Reprinted Edition of the San Lii Twu by the Jenq Family School in Shicherng].

[6] In the Syhbuh Tsorngkan (SBTK) collection (third series, printed 1936).

[7] See notes in Syhkuh Chyuanshu Tzoongmuh Tyiyaw (Commercial Press, four-volume ed.), I, 432–433.

[8] On the encyclopedia see Ssu-yu Teng and Knight Biggerstaff, An Annotated Bibliography of Selected Chinese Reference Works (rev. ed., Cambridge, Mass., 1950), p. 126.

The next surviving work listed in the *Sonq History*, *Hwangyow Shin Yueh Twujih* 皇祐新樂圖記 [Illustrations and Notes on the Newly Revised Music of the Hwangyow Reign], is a typical product of the musical controversies at court. Dissatisfied with previous reforms, Emperor Ren Tzong 仁宗 (reigned 1023–1064) ordered a further revision of the method of determining pitches. In 1053 a work embodying this reform was presented to the throne by the authors Roan Yih 阮逸 and Hwu Yuan 胡瑗. This *Twujih* is in three sections. The first begins with a description and criticism of a few palace bells and chimes which had irregular measurements. The authors then suggest the use of grains of millet as the standard of measurement for length, volume, and weight, with the application of these standards to the construction of pitch pipes. In the same section they deal with the numerical calculation for the twelve semitones in the octave, from one fundamental note, by the method of the so-called "Pythagorean cycle of fifths." The second section of the work gives details for casting new bells, cutting new stone chimes, and the proper order of hanging these in sets. The last section describes the large drum and the sacrificial vessels.

In 1239 a manuscript copy of this book was made from the original, which later disappeared. In 1806 a printed edition was made from the copy and included in the collection *Shyuejing Taoyuan*, which is available in many libraries today.[9]

The *Twujih* also relies upon ancient sources for authority. The dimensions of the bells and chimes are based on the *Jou Lii* [Rituals of the Jou Dynasty], and the use of grains of millet as the standard of measurement first appears in the "Monograph on Measure and Calendar" in the *Chyan Hann Shu* (History of the Former Hann Dynasty [206 B.C.–A.D. 8]).[10] Other works, such as the "Monograph on Measures and the Calendar" of the *How Hann Shu* (History of the Later Hann Dynasty [A.D. 25–221]),[11] and the *San Lii Twu* are frequently cited.

In spite of its imperial auspices, the *Twujih* did not settle the controversy, and the quarrels continued at court. The questions now concerned the width of the pitch pipes, types of millet, and whether the grains of millet were to be measured sidewise or lengthwise.[12] Even the eminent

---

[9] The *Tsorngshu Jyicherng* (*TSJC*) ed. (vol. 1671) is a 1937 photolith of the 1806 printing.

[10] By Ban Guh (A.D. 32–92), *et al.*, chaps. 21A and 21B. On this work and the following see Yang Liensheng, *Topics in Chinese History* (Cambridge, Mass., 1950), pp. 32–33.

[11] By Fann Yeh (A.D. 398–445), chaps. 11–13.

[12] *Syhkuh Chyuanshu Tzoongmuh Tyiyaw*, I, 793.

historian-statesman Symaa Guang (1019–1086) participated in a debate with one of the musical reformers, Fann Jenn 范鎮, over whether the pitch pipe of *hwang jong* should be defined as one with a length of ninety grains of millet or one with the volume of one thousand and two hundred grains of millet. Both prescriptions are given in the *History of the Former Hann Dynasty*.[13]

The third and largest of the Sonq works on music is the *Yueh Shu* 樂書 (Treatise on Music) by Chern Yang 陳暘, a conservative among musical scholars of the Northern Sonq period. The *Yueh Shu* was presented to the throne in 1104. Several copies of Sonq printings of the work survive to this day, either complete or in part. These and later editions are accessible in libraries in China and abroad.[14]

This work of two hundred chapters is in two main parts, chapters 1 to 108 and chapters 109 to 200. Chapters 1 to 95 consist of commentaries on practically all the passages in the Classics that mention musical matters.[15] In chapters 96 to 108 Chern Yang discusses standards of measurement and their application to musical instruments, the calculation of the twelve semitones, the five notes of the scale, and the significance of the eight "elements"—metal, stone, earth, leather, silk, bamboo, gourd, and wood—by which the musical instruments are grouped. In this section, again, philosophical discussion and allusions to the Classics outweigh factual information. Chapters 109 to 150, perhaps the most useful part of the book, contain listings of instruments under three main headings: "Yeayueh" 雅樂 (Ceremonial Music), "Hwuyueh" 胡樂 (Foreign Music), and "Swuyueh" 俗樂 (Popular Music), categories that are really more applicable to Tarng than to Sonq music.[16] Over half of

---

[13] See also Maa Duanlin, *Wenshiann Tongkao* (discussed below), 131.37–42.

[14] The collated edition of 1876 can be found in the Library of Congress and the Chinese-Japanese Library of Harvard-Yenching Institute at Harvard. The National Library of Peking has three editions: (1) a Sonq edition in 31 chapters; (2) an edition with woodblock cut in Sonq and printed in Yuan, in 66 chapters; (3) an edition with wood-block cut in Sonq and printed in Ming, in 84 chapters. All three are on microfilm in the Library of Congress.

A detailed account of the early printings of this work preserved in China and Japan is given by Taki Ryoichi in "Report on the Investigation of Chinese Musical Source Materials."

[15] These include the three Ritual collections, the *Classic of Songs*, the *Classic of Documents*, the *Spring and Autumn Annals* and its commentaries, the *Classic of Divination*, the *Classic of Filial Piety*, the *Analects* of Confucius, and the *Mencius*. On these canonical texts see Hightower, *Chinese Literature*, pp. 1–4; Yang, *Chinese History*, p. 41; and Charles S. Gardner, *Chinese Traditional Historiography* (second printing, Cambridge, Mass., 1961), p. 64.

[16] See Kishibe Shigeo, "A Short Bibliography on the Music of the Tarng Dynasty,"

the instruments mentioned are illustrated with woodcuts. The rest of the book deals with ritual and popular songs, various kinds of dances, and funeral and military music.

Most of the material upon which the *Yueh Shu* is based is still available. The work is most useful as a comprehensive review of Confucian theories of ceremonial music. Chern Yang himself presents very little that is unusual except his insistence on removing the two *biann* tones from the seven-note scale and keeping only the pentatonic scale (chapter 107). He also argues that since the series of semitones has only twelve notes, all the existing sets of bells and chimes which have sixteen members—the common size of sets used in Tarng times—should be reduced to twelve (even when the four extra bells are merely octave duplications of the first four semitones—chapter 112). It must be remembered that although the book is a work of the latter part of the Northern Sonq, in general Chern Yang draws heavily upon Tarng dynasty sources,[17] so that it is not primarily an account of contemporary Sonq music.

An important difference between this work and the two previous works is that Chern Yang took the trouble to include illustrations[18] of instruments used for the foreign and popular music about which he frequently makes disparaging remarks. Occasionally in this section one also finds mention of interesting current musical practices. For example, he says that there was still in use in Sonq times a certain kind of *bann-tzyh puu* 半字譜 (half-character notation) inherited from the court entertainment music of the Tarng dynasty. As a matter of fact, the Duen-hwang *pyiba* notation representing Tarng entertainment music does actually look like fragments of Chinese characters.[19] And in chapter 148 Chern Yang makes the earliest mention of the use of a thin membrane to cover a hole on the horizontal flute—a device still found on the flute today—which gives the instrument its distinctive timbre.

Despite its comprehensiveness, Chern Yang's work was not well received when he presented it to the throne.[20] The reason might be found in the political background of the time. In the reign of Emperor

---

p. 73.

[17] See Kishibe Shigeo, "A Historical Study on the Twenty-eight Modes of the Popular Music in the Tang Period," p. 450.

[18] Some are inaccurate, for example, in chapter 129 the label for a lute is "chou pyiba wuushyan" 搊琵琶五絃 (hand-plucked lute, five strings), but the illustration shows only four strings and four pegs.

[19] The Sonq poet-musician Jiang Kwei (see below) also mentions in his preface to his *tsyr* melody No. 3 a *pyiba* notation existing in his time and specified that it was a tablature.

[20] *Sonq History*, 432.5593a.

Huei Tzong 徽宗 (1101–1126) there was a continual power struggle between the progressive and the conservative factions in the government. The emperor's favor shifted frequently from one to the other. Even musical matters were the subject of dispute. Just at this time the emperor was engrossed in the proposal of the Taoist Wey Hannjin 魏漢津 who suggested using the measurements of certain of the emperor's fingers as the standard in regulating the length of pitch pipes.[21]

Although Chern Yang's work did not impress the emperor, it became highly regarded by Confucian scholars, who deserve credit for its preservation. Almost one hundred years later, in 1202, on the occasion of a reprinting of the *Yueh Shu,* a Southern Sonq scholar, Lou Yueh 樓鑰 (1137–1213), compiled a table of corrigenda to it which he called *Yueh Shu Jenqwuh* 樂書正誤, containing over three hundred entries, most of which are scribal errors.[22]

We must resort to the chronicle in the *Sonq History* to discover what happened on the musical scene between Chern Yang's work (1104) and the downfall of the Northern Sonq dynasty (1127), since today there is no work extant dealing at first hand with the music of this period. In 1105 Tsay Jing 蔡京, the powerful minister who was responsible for recommending the Taoist Wey Hannjing to the emperor, founded a new musical institution called the Dahshenq Fuu 大晟府, which dominated the musical scene for the next twenty years. However, because of the unorthodoxy of some of Tsay's and Wey's ideas and perhaps even more the ill repute of these two men,[23] historians and later scholars generally denounced their musical activities.[24] From the *Sonq History* and other historical works[25] we know the names of musicians employed by the

[21] *Sonq History,* 128.4790d.

[22] A Sonq printing of the corrigenda exists in the National Peking Library in Taiwan, and there is a *Tzershyhjiu Tsorngshu* edition, 1913–1916 (fasc. no. 11), which is a fascimile of a different Sonq printing.

[23] According to Wey's biography in the *Sonq History,* 462.5658c, he was a *chyngtzwu* 黥卒, a soldier whose face had been branded. Tsay Jing's (1046–1126) biography in *Sonq History,* 476.5678a-d, appears under the heading "Traitorous Ministers." See also Herbert A. Giles, *A Chinese Biographical Dictionary* (London and Shanghai, 1898), pp. 748-749.

[24] A comprehensive study of this institution was made by Ling Jiingyan in an article (with English summary) entitled "The Music of Wei Han-ching and the Ta-shenq Institute of the Sung Dynasty", 1940. Lii Wenyuh in his "Dahshenq Fuu Kaoliueh" [Outline Study of the Dahshenq Institute], 1935, has a more favorable view of the influences of the Dahshenq Institute.

[25] For example, *Sonq Hueyyaw Gao, Yuh Hae,* and *Wenshiann Tongkao,* all of which will be discussed later.

Dahshenq Fuu and the titles of many books written on Dahshenq Fuu music. A book called *Yueh Shu Ba Luenn* 樂書八論 [Eight Discourses on Music] was written on imperial order in 1111 by Liou Biing 劉昺, one of the most prolific writers on the subject. It is lost, but is quoted at some length in the *Sonq History*.[26]

After 1127, when the Northern Sonq capital was captured and all institutions connected with ceremonial music were destroyed, together with the books and instruments, the state of music at the new Southern court reverted to conditions at the beginning of the dynasty.[27] During the early years of the Southern Sonq, ceremonial music in the court revived very slowly. Scholars continued to offer suggestions to the emperor for finding the appropriate music for court functions, as for example Jiang Kwei (of whom more later) in his *Dahyueh Yih* 大樂議 [Expounding the Great Music], which is partially preserved through quotations in the *Sonq History*.[28]

The first major musical treatise of the Southern Sonq is *Liuhleu Shin Shu* 律呂新書 [A New Treatise on the Pitch Pipes] by Tsay Yuandinq 蔡元定 (1135–1198). The preface (1187) was written by the philosopher Ju Shi 朱熹, who was Tsay's strong supporter and friend. It was through Ju Shi's recommendation that the work was presented to the throne. Little is known about the early printings of the book. In 1415 it was incorporated into *Shinqlii Dahchyuan* 性理大全, a collection of philosophical items done on imperial order.[29] In addition, the annotations of the Ming scholar Harn Bangchyi 韓邦奇 (1479–1555)[30] and the Ching scholar Uang Shiuan 汪烜 (1692–1759)[31] have helped to preserve Tsay's

---

[26] 129,4791b-c.

[27] *Ibid.*

[28] Chap. 131.

[29] See Bartlett Wu, K. T. "Books on East Asiatic Music in the Library of Congress (Compiled before 1800)," p. 124. Sixteenth-century printings of the *Shinqlii Dahchyuan* are available both in the Library of Congress and in the Chinese-Japanese Library of the Harvard-Yenching Institute.

[30] His version is *Yuanluoh Jyh Yueh* 苑洛志樂 of *Yuanluoh's Book of Music* (see Bartlett-Wu, p. 125), Yuanluoh being one of the names by which Tsay Yuandinq was known. The 1806 reprinting issued as *Gongjean Gong Jyh Yueh* 恭簡公志樂 uses an honorific posthumous title for the author.

[31] In his *Yueh Jing Liuhleu Tongjiee* 樂經律呂通解 [Comprehensive Annotations on the Classic of Music (in the Collected Ritual) and (the Book on) the Pitch Pipes]. A small portion of Tsay's work is missing in this book. The *TSJC* edition is a reprint of another edition with a colophon dated 1862. There is a Wuhyuan Shiann 婺源縣 edition dated 1883.

work. Their annotated editions are now more easily accessible than *Shinqlii Dahchyuan*.

The twenty-three chapters of Tsay Yuandinq's book are grouped in two sections. The first consists of the presentation of the scheme of eighteen notes with numerical calculations, the formation of sixty possible modes using these notes, and the standards of measurement. The second section consists of citations from earlier histories and the Classics to support the author's theses.

Like many earlier musical theorists, Tsay Yuandinq was greatly interested in constructing scales of identical intervallic pattern on each of the twelve pitches. The difficulty lies in that the twelve notes obtained by the Pythagorean cycle of fifths do not form a closed circle. (The twelfth fifth is twenty-four cents higher than the octave of the first note.) To form identical scales beginning on each of the twelve pitches, one needs to add six more notes (obtained by the same cyclical method) to the basic twelve semitones.[32] But this group of eighteen notes lacks symmetry in that the six extra notes cannot be used on all scales. From the Hann period on, much attention had been given to this problem but no satisfactory solution was found until the mathematical solution of the equal-tempered chromatic scale of prince Ju Tzayyuh of the Ming dynasty. Tsay's suggestion is to forget about the relationship among the notes within the group of pitches and to simply adopt the eighteen notes necessary for the scales. (See Table 4 in Chapter II.) Another feature of this treatise is the first use of the terms *chii-diaw* 起調 (to begin the mode) and *bih-cheu* 畢曲 (to end the piece) for each mode, with the notes specified.[33] The idea, however, is not entirely new, for the term *shasheng* 殺聲 (ending note) already existed in the late eleventh century.[34]

Tsay Yuandinq was not helped by Ju Shi's endorsement of his theories.[35] On the contrary, it may have been directly detrimental to Tsay's

---

[32] For a succinct description of the scales in the form of a chart, see Wang Guangchyi, *History of Chinese Music*, I. 88. The eighteen notes when brought within the octave are: c, g, d, a, e, b, f-sharp, c-sharp, g-sharp, d-sharp, a-sharp, f, c-plus, g-plus, d-plus, e-plus, e-plus, b-plus ("plus" meaning 24 cents higher). Tsay uses the prefix *biann* 變 to designate the "plus" notes, which are different from the two so-called *biann*-tones in the seven-note diatonic scale.

[33] The meaning of the term *chii-diaw* 起調 has been debated by several later writers. The musical examples from Sonq show that this applies more often to the end of the first or second phrase than to the initial note of a piece.

[34] In Sheen Gua 沈括, *Memoirs at Menqshi*, pars. 532, 541. See discussion of this work below.

[35] On Ju Shi's estimation of Tsay see his *Collected Discourses*, 92.96.

position, for Ju Shi himself was involved in political disputes. In 1196, when Ju's opponent in court purged him from office, Tsay was also accused of heresy and banished to Chongling 舂陵 (in Central China), where he died soon after.[36] But as shown in many subsequent works on music,[37] his theories gained lasting attention. The writers of the *Sonq History* already speak favorably of him.

Ju Shi 朱熹 (1130–1200),[38] China's most celebrated philosophical syncretist, was a scholar with very wide interests and a prolific writer. His posthumously published *Yilii Jing juann Tong jiee* 儀禮經傳通解 (A General Survey of Ritual)[39] contains three sections dealing with music. Two of these, sections 22 and 23 in chapter 13, concern the pitch pipe and the scale system; the other, section 24 in chapter 14, contains musical settings, written in the *liuhleu* 律呂 notation,[40] of twelve poems from the *Classic of Poetry,* for ritual purposes.

The *Yilii Jing juann Tong jiee* was first printed between 1217 and 1222, and a copy of this edition is now in the National Central Library in Taiwan.[41] There are also a Japanese edition of 1662 and several Chinese editions printed between 1831 and 1850. The musical settings of the twelve poems have often been reproduced in other works, notably in the *Seh Puu,* which will be discussed below, and in the *Yueh Dean* 樂典 [Canons of Music] by Hwang Tzuoo 黃佐 (1490–1566);[42] and a carefully collated edition can be found in *Sheng Liuh Tongkao* 聲律通考 [A Historical Investigation of the Scale System] by Chern Lii 陳澧 (1810–1882).[43]

It is not necessary to comment here on Ju Shi's unsurpassed influence on the intellectual history of China. His interpretations of the Classics were accepted as authoritative by later generations of scholars, and his writings on ceremonial music also carried much prestige. In the *Tong jiee* he contributed little that was original, merely making a summary of

---

[36] On Ju Shi, see *Sonq History,* 429.5585a; on Tsay, *ibid.,* 434.5595d. See also "Monograph on Measurement and Calendar" in *Sonq History,* 81.4682c.

[37] For example, those mentioned in notes 29–31 above.

[38] See note 36, and Fung Yu-lan, "Chu Hsi's Philosophy," *HJAS,* 7 (1942): 1–51.

[39] I am adopting the paraphrased translation given by Laurence Picken, in his study of this work, "Twelve Ritual Melodies of the T'ang Dynasty."

[40] For an explanation of this notation see Chapter III.

[41] In the microfilm copy of this edition the music section—especially the musical notes—shows some emendations by a later hand of unknown date.

[42] In 36 chapters, printed 1682. See also Bartlett-Wu, "Books on East Asiatic Music," p. 125.

[43] Printed by the author in Panyeu 番禺 (that is, Canton), 1858.

earlier commentaries on the *Classic of Ceremony and Ritual*. However, it may have been his inclusion of Tsay Tuandinq's theory of eighteen notes[44] which influenced later scholar's interest in Tsay's work. As for the twelve songs, Ju Shi noted that they were not in style in his time,[45] and that they were cited from a collection made by one Jaw Yannsuh 趙彥肅 (ca. 1170), who claimed that the songs dated back to the Kaiyuan (713–741) period of the Tarng. Laurence Picken[46] also found in these songs certain musical features which argue in favor of their pre-Sonq or Tarng origin. On the other hand the characteristics which he pointed out can all be found in a more popular genre, the *tsyr* songs, by Jiang Kwei, a poet-musician born twenty-five years after Ju Shi.[47] Whatever the origin of these twelve ritual songs, it was Ju Shi who provided a precedent for countless similar musical compositions by later Confucian musicians,[48] the earliest example of which is to be found in the next and last work to be classed here as a theoretical treatise.

Shyong Pernglai 熊朋來, who produced the *Seh Puu* 瑟譜 [Music of the Twenty-five-stringed Zither], was in his thirties in 1279 when the Sonq dynasty fell and the Mongols took over all of China.[49] The short introductory treatise in his book discusses the tuning system (the *seh* played entirely on open strings with movable bridges), the sixty modes of Tsay Yuandinq, the classical and popular systems of notation, and some details of playing technique. The main body consists of the words

---

[44] Sec. 23, chap. 13.

[45] Chap. 14, sec. 24. Yang Yinnliou, in his *Outline History of Chinese Music*, p. 192, doubts their Tarng origin.

[46] *Twelve Ritual Melodies* (pp. 170, 171, 173). Besides the transcription by Picken, the Ritual Songs have also been transcribed into the *gongcheh* notation (discussed below, Chap. III) by Day Charnggeng in his book *Talks on Music,* II. 59. For other interpretations of these songs, see below, Chaps. III and IV.

[47] This is true both in their close adherence to the Sonq dynasty modal theory and in other interesting musical features. For example, the underlying pentatonic structure in many of the heptatonic melodies (Picken, *Twelve Ritual Melodies*, p. 173; below, Chap. III, p. 67; the use of the *shang* mode with the final cadence in the upper octave (Picken, p. 171; Chap. II, Table 3); the use of stock melodies within the same mode (picken, p. 168; Chap. I, Table 1); intermodal borrowing of melodic materials (Picken, p. 169; Chap. IV, notes to number 16;) and the emphasis on the interval of the third in the *gong* (fa) melodies and the emphasis on the fourth in the *shang* (sol) melodies (Picken, p. 167; Chap. III).

[48] On composers from the thirteenth to the eighteenth centuries who composed music of a similar type, see Yang Yinnliou, *History*, pp. 192–201.

[49] His biography in *Yuan History*, 190.6563c, gives no dates for his birth and death; Jiang Lianqfu's *Lihday Renwuh Nianlii Beijuann Tzonqbeau* (1961, Hongkong edition) gives 1246–1323.

and music of forty-three songs, some of them many stanzas long, to be sung with *seh* accompaniment. Each song is given once in the classical *liuhleu* notation and once in the *gongcheh* notation.[50] The first twelve pieces duplicate those in Ju Shi's collection. Of the remainder, twenty-two are Shyong's own settings of other texts from the *Classic of Poetry* and nine are his settings of hymns for specific services in the Confucian temple. The concluding chapter consists of classical allusions to the *seh*.

In 1408 the *Seh Puu* was incorporated in manuscript form into the great imperial Ming collection *Yeongleh Dahdean*, and from this copies were made for the *Syhkuh Chyuanshu* (1788).[51] Today, many editions of the *Seh Puu* are available.[52]

Shyong Pernglai's thesis is that the *seh* should be the sole insturment used in accompanying the singing of ritual songs. Although Shyong lived into the Yuan period, his work reflects the spirit of Ju Shi's teaching to the point of imitating the style of the twelve ritual songs in his own compositions.[53] Shyong notes Tsay Yuandinq's system of modulation, but his incomplete description of the sixty modes derived from the modulation leads one to suspect that he does not really understand Tsay's theory. In fact, many of his compositions show that his concept of modes in general is by no means clear.[54] Besides advocating the use of the *seh*, Shyong insists on a chromatic tuning of its twenty-five strings. For this, he cites some passages of the Classics. Other Sonq and later scholars, however, also found support in the Classics for their belief that the *seh* should be tuned pentatonically.[55]

When the Mongol regime came into power and solicited the services of eminent scholars, Shyong refused to serve the new dynasty and retired to his home town, where he taught the Classics privately.[56]

[50] For a discussion of these systems of notation see below, Chap. III. A transcription of the seventh melody, "Fartarn" 伐檀, with Yang Yinnliou's own rhythmic interpretations, appears in *Photographic Illustrations of Musical Materials for Study of the History of Chinese Music*, ed. Yang, et al. (1955), vol. 5, *notes*, p. 14.

[51] See *Syhkuh Tyiyaw*, I, 793.

[52] In the first half of the nineteenth century, three editions of the *Seh Puu* were made: the *Mohhae Jinhwu* 墨海金壺 edition (1812, 1921); the *Jyy Hae* 指海 edition (1837); and the *Jing Yuan* 經苑 edition (1847), which is based on a draft copy of the 1788 version. The TSJC and the Dahdong Book Company editions, both made in 1936, are photolithographic copies of the *Jyy Hae* edition. The Yuehyeatarng 粵雅堂 edition (1852) is a new printing based upon the *Jing Yuan* edition.

[53] See Shyong's own comment on this in his introduction to *Seh Puu*.

[54] See my notes to transcriptions of Shyong's ceremonial songs in Chap. IV.

[55] For more details on this controversy see *Syhkuh Tyiyaw*, I.793.

[56] *Yuan History*, 190.6563c.

Historical and Encyclopedic Compilations

We have already seen that several treatises on music have been preserved through copious quotations in the *Sonq History* which, like the other dynastic histories, is essentially a collection of official and other documents of the period, edited by scholars of the succeeding dynasty. The encyclopedias and other kinds of historical compilation are also invaluable depositories of texts that otherwise are no longer extant.[57] Included here are some outstanding Sonq compilations with sections on music, of which only the last is a work devoted entirely to musical subjects.

The first work in this group, *Sonq Hueyyaw* 宋會要 [A Compilation of State Regulations of Sonq], has a rather complicated history. It is a collection of documents relating to institutions of the Sonq dynasty, written during various reigns of that dynasty by many different historians.[58] The *Hueyyaw* as it appears today is an 1809 restoration from manuscript copies of parts of the original,[59] with the reassembled mass of material never thoroughly edited.[60]

In its present form the *Hueyyaw* is divided into four hundred and

[57] On encyclopedias see Teng and Biggerstaff, *Annotated Bibliography*, pp. 106–107; on histories see Gardner, *Chinese Traditional Historiography*, pp. 87–97; Yang, *Chinese History*, p. 32; and H. H. Dubs, "The Reliability of Chinese Histories," *Far Eastern Quarterly*, 6 (1946): 23–43. I have not included here the ten or more Sonq dynasty encyclopedic works which contain mostly quotations of musical writings dated before the Sonq, since many of the works quoted still exist independently. Most of these encyclopedias add little to the factual information on music of the Sonq period, but they do indicate the type of musical writings read by the literate musicians of the time. In 1962 a compilation entitled *Jonggwo Guuday Inyueh Shyyliaw Jyiyaw* 中國古代音樂史料輯要 [Selections of Ancient Chinese Musical Historical Sources] was made by the Institute for the Study of Chinese Music 中國音樂研究所 of the Central Academy of Music 中央音樂學院 in Peking, bringing together by photocopying method musical materials in encyclopedias 類書 dating from the Swei through the Ching period. Of the twenty-six titles included, twelve are from the Sonq (pp. 687–725).

[58] Teng and Biggerstaff, pp. 162–163; Edward A. Kracke, Jr., *Civil Service in Early Sung China* (Harvard-Yenching Institute Monograph Series, XIV; Cambridge, Mass., 1953), pp. 244–245.

[59] According to Tang Jong 湯中 who in *Sonq Hueyyaw Yanjiou* (Shanghai, 1931) made a thorough study of the work, ten *hueyyaw* are known to have been written covering the years from the beginning of the Sonq dynasty in 960 to 1225. During the early Ming dynasty, between 1403 and 1425, seven of the *hueyyaw* were broken up and copied into the great imperial encyclopedia *Yeongleh Dahdean*. By the time Shyu Song 徐松 in 1809 undertook to reassemble all these *hueyyaw* by copying the parts out of the *Yeongleh Dahdean*, the originals had long since disappeared.

[60] The photolithographic copy done in 1936 by the Dahdong Book Company makes

sixty chapters, arranged by categories.[61] The music section (chapters 95–102) has the following headings:

Chapter 95: Pitch Pipes

Chapter 96: Pitch Pipes (continued)

Chapter 97: The Pitches; Musical Events of the Sonq Dynasty

Chapter 98: Musical Instruments; Ceremonial Dances; State Sacrifices and Worship

Chapter 99: State Sacrifices and Worship; Musical Settings of the Poems in the *Book of Poetry:* the Conservatory

Chapter 100: Ritual Songs for the Various Sacrifices

Chapter 101: Ritual Songs for the Temple Sacrifices

Chapter 102: Military and Processional Songs.

The actual content of the chapters, however, is not so clearly organized. At the beginning of chapter 97, for instance, there is a list of instruments used in the court orchestra which logically belongs under the heading of chapter 98. On the other hand, the section that actually begins chapter 98 seems to be a continuation of events discussed at the end of chapter 97. A large section of chapter 98 (pages 18a–19b) is almost an exact duplication of another section in chapter 96 (pages 21a–22b). Furthermore there are many unconnected sections and short paragraphs that are not integrated into the text at all.[62]

This restored work also draws upon books of later date. For example, in the music sections there are often marginal labels which are actually chapter headings used in the *Sonq History*.[63] For these reasons the work is also known as *Sonq Hueyyaw Gao* 宋會要稿 [Draft *Sonq Hueyyaw*]. Obviously it presents problems to the user and he must be constantly on guard for scribal errors.[64] Nevertheless it is an extremely important

---

use of Shyu Song's original manuscript with the notes and corrections of various editors interlined and in the margins.

[61] A table of the contents (120 pages) of the *Sonq Hueyyaw*, prepared by Liou Cherng-gann 劉承幹, is appended at the end of Tang Jong's book.

[62] For example, 95.23, 97.3–4.

[63] For example, 97.1a and 2b, 樂志, the "Monograph on Music," and 律曆志, the "Monograph on Measurements and Calendar." Another curious label, *Chyuan Tarng Wen* 全唐文, appears in the margin of the *Sonq Hueyyaw*, because the latter work was restored during the compilation of the *Chyuan Tarng Wen* from fragments preserved in the *Yeongleh Dahdean* (see note 59 above).

[64] For example, a comparison of the two duplicated passages mentioned earlier with the identical passage in the *Sonq History* (chap. 127) shows that all three versions differ from each other in small details. For further criticisms of the *Sonq Hueyyaw* see Tang Jong's study (note 59 above), 3.8–9.

source. Its materials were drawn upon for the compilation of the official *Sonq History*, in which they are frequently much condensed. For instance, the *Hueyyaw* gives a much better account of the contention between the ministers Sonq Chyi 宋祁 and Lii Jaw 李照 over the total number of bells and chimes that should be hung in the orchestra (chapter 95, page 116), and a more detailed listing of the number of musicians who had to be dismissed from each instrumental group of the court orchestra during a period of retrenchment early in the Southern Sonq (chapter 99, page 8a). In the *Hueyyaw* one finds also many interesting details which are not mentioned at all in the official history, including an account of the request made by an official named Ju Wei 朱維 in 1113 to put labels indicating pitch on every single bell, chime, and pipe (of the mouth organ, and so forth) of the orchestra—even next to the holes of the ocarina—in order to facilitate learning the newly established Dahshenq music (chapter 98, page 1a); and from 1141 an account of another official, Jou Lin 周林, who requested that the bell and chime players perform standing up because ordinary chairs should not be placed among the sacred objects.[65]

A word must be said also about the extensive section on the Bureaucracy ("Jyrguan Jyh" 職官志, chapters 144–238), which deals with the organization and the operation of the government, since many musical functions in the court were actually part of government. Included in this section are records concerning such institutions as the Bureau of Bells and Drums (Jongguu Yuann 鐘鼓院), in chapters 169 and 180; and the Court of Imperial Sacrifices (Taycharng Syh 太常寺), the Dahshenq Institute, the Conservatory of Music (Jiaw Fang 教坊), the Bureau of Ceremonial Music (Dahyueh Jyu 大樂局), and the Bureau of Military Music (Guuchuei Jyu 鼓吹局), all in chapter 171. The importance of this section as a source for musical activities in the Sonq court needs no elaboration.

Sonq Shyy 宋史, the official *Sonq History*, has already been referred to many times. This work, traditionally said to have been edited by the Mongol Tuotuo 托托 (ca. early fourteenth century?) and the Chinese Ouyang Shyuan 歐陽玄 (1274/5–1358) but actually edited by the latter alone, was completed in 1345 and printed promptly.[66]

---

[65] 98.3a. The other instrumentalists performed while sitting on the ground.

[66] Among the many editions today, the *Bornah* edition is a photolithographic copy of the 1345 printing with some restorations taken from the 1480 edition. An outstanding later printing is the carefully prepared Palace edition commissioned by the Emperor

The *Sonq History* totals 496 chapters. The "Yueh Jyh" 樂志 (Monograph on Music) is seventeen chapters long (126–142). Its contents can be described as follows:

Chapters 126–131: A strictly chronological presentation of various kinds of musical events at the court

Chapters 132–141: Texts of hymns for various ceremonies

Chapters 142: Discussion of Ju Shi's songs from the *Book of Poetry*, the tuning of the zither, the scales of popular music, music and dances for entertainment, and military music.

The *Sonq Shyy* is not considered one of the best of the dynastic histories. The compilers have been accused of bias as well as uncritical use of source materials,[67] and the work abounds in factual errors.[68] Be that as it may, it contains a wealth of material conveniently assembled.

The "Monograph on Music" is arranged partly chronologically and partly topically. In the first six chapters such topics as the problem of constructing pitch pipes, the prescribed sequence of the ceremonial dances, and the seating arrangement of the instrumentalists interrupt the year by year chronicle of musical events.

A very useful portion of the *Sonq History* is the enormous biographical section. It includes, to name only a few of the most important musical figures, biographies of the court theorists Her Shean 和峴 (chapter 444) and Hwu Yuan 胡瑗 (chapter 432); the eminent scholars Nieh Chorngyih 聶崇義 (chapter 431) and Ju Shi 朱熹 (chapter 429); lesser known but important writers on music such as Chern Yang 陳暘 (chapter 432) and Tsay Yuandinq 蔡元定 (chapter 434); and the colorful figure Wey Hannjin 魏漢津 (chapter 462). Many other sections in the *Sonq History* contain relevant materials for the study of music history. The annals of the reign of each emperor such as that of Emperor Huei Tzong (chapters 19–22) record major musical events which took place at court. The "Liuhlih Jyh" 律曆志 [Monograph on Measurement and the Calendar] contains a passage from the lost musical treatise *Jiingyow Yueh Swei Shin Jing* 景祐樂髓新經. Although the quotation is quite short it is a vital source on the modes of popular music in the Northern Sonq period

Chyanlung, and presented to him in 1747. A facsimile printing of this Palace edition was made in 1894 by the Torngwen (同文) Book Company and a photolithographic copy in 1934 by the Kaiming Book Company.

[67] Liang Chiichau, "Wang Jinggong Juann—fuh *Sonq Shyy* Sypyng" 王荊公傳—附宋史私評 [A Biography of Wang Anshyr, with an Appendix of Some Informal Criticisms of the *Sonq History*], *Yiinbingshyh Tsorngjiuh* 飲冰室叢著, I.4, pp. 9–13.

[68] *Syhkuh Tyiyaw*, II.1008–1010.

[15]

(chapter 71, page 4654d).[69] In the "Jyrguan Jyh" 職官志 [Monograph on the Organization and Operation of the Government], chapter 164, page 4877d, we find recorded the establishment of the musical institute Dahshenq Fuu with descriptions of its administrative details. In the "Yihwen Jyh" 藝文志 [Monograph on Bibliography], chapter 202, page 4987c–d, there is a list of over one hundred books on music which were extant during the Sonq dynasty.[70]

We now come to an encyclopedia of general knowledge called *Yuh Hae* 玉海 [literally, the Jade Sea].[71] This was compiled by the scholar Wang Inglin 王應麟 (1223–1296), and is in two hundred chapters, covering the periods from ancient times to the end of the Sonq dynasty. The encyclopedia was first printed between 1337 and 1340 and several copies of the original edition still exist.[72]

The music section of the *Jade Sea* encyclopedia is organized as follows:

Chapters 103–105: General Music Events
Chapter 106: Ceremonial Hymns
Chapter 107: Ceremonial Dances
Chapter 108: Music of the Border Areas
Chapter 109: Wind and Percussion Instruments, and so forth
Chapter 110: Stringed Instruments, Drums and other miscellaneous Instruments.

Each of these topics is treated chronologically, but in most cases the Sonq period occupies a substantial portion. It is to be noted that the specialized topic of pitch pipes is not mentioned under "Music" at all but only under "Measurement and the Calendar" (chapters 6 and 7), which is located in another section of the encyclopedia.

---

[69] Written under the name of the Emperor Ren Tzong 仁宗 in 1035. For its significance see Chapter II on the Sonq dynasty modal system. Contents of this work are listed in the *Yuh Hae* encyclopedia, chapter 7, and in the *Wenshiann Tongkao*, chapter 130, both to be discussed below.

[70] For Chinese comments on this bibliography and a list of supplements to chapter 202 by later writers, see Nieh Chorngchyi 聶崇岐, "Preface to *Combined Indices to Twenty Historical Bibliographies*" (Harvard-Yenching Institute Sinological Index Series, no. 10, Peiping, 1933), p. 5.

[71] See Robert des Rotours, *Le Traité des examens traduit de la nouvelle histoire des T'ang* (Paris, 1932), pp. 96–97; Teng and Biggerstaff, *Annotated Bibliography*, pp. 122–123.

[72] They are listed in the *Union Catalogue of Nationally Owned Sonq and Yuan Editions in Taiwan* 台灣公藏宋元本聯合書目 compiled by Chang Biider 昌彼得 and published by the National Central Library, Taipei, 1955, Among later and easily available editions are the two Ching printings done by Kang Jityan 康基田 in 1806 and by the Jehjiang Book Company in 1883.

The *Jade Sea,* which was designed for students planning to take the special examination for documentary experts during the Sonq dynasty,[73] is remarkable for the wealth of materials cited. Although the total number of works appearing in the music section is smaller than the list given in the "Monograph on Bibliography" of the *Sonq History,* only about one half of the *Jade Sea* list overlaps that of the *Sonq History.* The author is quite liberal in supplying notes for the musical treatises listed, though he keeps his critical opinions to a minimum. Besides giving detailed lists of contents, he sometimes describes the occasion on which a certain treatise was commissioned[74] or the nature of the revision of a certain work.[75] Incomplete editions are noted,[76] and when different bibliographies give variant descriptions of a certain work (for example, in the numbering of chapters), Wang Inglin takes them all into account.[77]

A final word should be said about the sources of the *Jade Sea* encyclopedia, which the compiler never fails to indicate clearly each time they are quoted. Some of these are famous bibliographies from the Sonq period, such as *Chorngwen Tzoongmuh* 崇文總目[78] and *Jiunjai Dwushu Jyh* 郡齋讀書志.[79] Other works utilized by Wang include important official records which eventually went into the compilation of the *Sonq History,* such as the *Hueyyaw* already discussed and the *Shyrluh* 實録 [Veritable Records] of various reigns.[80]

The fourth work in this group of encyclopedias, the *Wenshiann Tongkao* 文獻通考 [A Comprehensive Investigation of Documents and Traditions],[81] is an encyclopedia of Chinese institutions compiled by Maa Duanlin 馬端臨, who lived at the end of the Sonq and the beginning of the Yuan dynasty. The work was completed sometime before 1319. Several Yuan (1279–1368) printings, some complete and some incomplete, as well as many Ming printings from Yuan and Ming blocks, are

---

[73] Kracke, *Civil Service,* p. 248.

[74] See 105.32–35b on the compilation of the *Jiingyow Goangyueh Jih* 景祐廣樂記.

[75] See 105.45a on the revision of the *Yueh Shu* 樂書 by Fann Jenn 范鎮.

[76] See 105.35b for a descriptiou of *Yueh Jih* 樂記 by Wn Liangfuu 吳良輔.

[77] 105.44a, gives descriptions of Fann Jenn's *Yueh Shu* from three different sources.

[78] Partially restored in the eighteenth century; see Teng and Biggerstaff, *Annotated Bibliography,* pp. 18–19. In the *Jade Sea* it is often referred to as *Chorngwen Muh.*

[79] In the *Jade Sea* it is often referred to as *Chaur Shyh Jyh* 晁氏志; see Teng and Biggerstaff, p. 19.

[80] On the various *Shyrluh* as historical sources see Bernard S. Solomon, *The Veritable Record of the T'ang Emperor Shun-tsung* (Cambridge, Mass., 1955), pp. xxiii-xxiv.

[81] See Des Rotours, *Nouvelle histoire des T'ang,* pp. 87–89; Teng and Biggerstaff, *Annotated Bibliography,* pp. 150–151.

still extant today in China and Japan.[82]

Of the 348 chapters in this encyclopedia, 21 (chapters 128–148) are devoted to music. The contents of these are described as follows:

Chapters 128–130: A chronological account of musical events in the court

Chapter 131: A chronological account of the constructing of pitch pipes

Chapter 132: An entire section on determining the pitches of bells, taken from Ju Shi's *Ju Huey'an Yilii Jingjuann Tongjiee*

Chapter 133: A chronological account of attempts at obtaining a standard mensuration

Chapters 134–139: A comprehensive list of musical instruments arranged by the eight traditional categories of materials plus one supplementary group, each of which is subdivided into three sections: ceremonial, foreign, and popular musical instruments

Chapter 140: Seating arrangements for the various types of orchestras

Chapters 141–143: Vocal music for ceremonies and entertainment

Chapters 144–145: Ceremonial dances

Chapter 146: Music and dances of foreign origin for entertainment

Chapter 147: Vaudeville Entertainment

Chapter 148: Music of the border areas and music for the conclusion of certain ceremonies.

In addition there is a bibliographical section (chapter 168) which contains a descriptive list of seventy-five works on music.

The *Wenshiann Tongkao* contains both important documents and worthwhile commentaries, which Maa Duanlin differentiates very clearly in his texts. On Sonq music there are pieces of information that do not appear in any of the other three works mentioned above. One example concerns the tuning and position of the frets of the five-stringed lute (chapter 137, page 35a–b) and the thirteen-stringed zither (chapter 137, page 37a). On the controversy over the different methods of using grains of millet to measure the size of the pitch pipe, Maa Duanlin quotes the entire correspondence between the leaders of the two opposing camps, Symaa Guang 司馬光 and Fann Jenn 范鎮 (chapter

---

[82] The copy preserved in the Palace Museum in Taiwan is a Ming printing from blocks that were cut in 1324. The editions commonly used by present-day scholars are the Palace blockprint edition of 1747, the photolithographic copy of this edition done by the Commercial Press in 1936, and the Jehjiang Book Company edition of 1896.

131, page 37a–42b). It is a little disappointing that the section on instruments is mostly borrowed from Chern Yang's *Yueh Shu* (but without the illustrations). Even Chern Yang's opinions, such as his disapproval of the use of the *biann* tones in the scale, of the use of seven strings on the zither (chapter 137, page 13a), and of the adoption of foreign instruments (chapter 138, page 21a), are transferred intact from Chern Yang's book. And Maa repeats Chern Yang's mistake in dividing the instruments into the three categories, ceremonial, foreign, and popular—a system of organization which is not typical of the Sonq orchestra,[83] as noted before.

The *Tongkao* is on the whole a highly esteemed work because of Maa Duanlin's keen criticisms and interpretations.[84] Though not a music specialist, his observations on the court controversies over musical matters (pitch regulation, for example) are penetrating. After summarizing the accounts of the six musical reforms, Maa notes that after at least three of the reforms the performing musicians of the court quietly altered the new regulations to suit their own convenience.[85]

The last of these compilations is a much smaller work, the *Chyn Shyy* 琴史 [History of the Chyn][86] by Ju Charngwen 朱長文 (1041–1100), a book of short biographies of 146 persons connected with the *chyn,* arranged in chronological order. Most of the names are from ancient or legendary times: 57 from the pre-Hann period, 56 from the beginning of Hann to the end of Swei, and 24 from the Tarng. Only 9 are from the Northern Sonq. These biographies comprise five of the six chapters of the book. The last chapter deals with the tuning and the dimensions of the *chyn,* the significance of each note in the scale, and so forth.[87]

The author's preface is dated 1084, but the book was not printed until 1233, when his grandnephew Suen Jenqdah 孫正大 undertook the project and added another preface to it. In the eighteenth and nineteenth centuries we find manuscript copies of this work listed in the catalogues of several rare book libraries.[88] The only available edition today is the

[83] See above, note 16.

[84] Teng and Biggerstaff, *Annotated Bibliography,* p. 151.

[85] 130.13b–14b.

[86] Van Gulik translates the title as "History of the Lute" in his *The Lore of the Chinese Lute,* p. 167.

[87] Van Gulik's translation (*ibid.*) of the items in this chapter is as follows: (1) sonorous tubes; (2) strings; (3) dimensions; (4) form (of the instrument); (5) tones; (6) modes; (7) songs; (8) manufacture; (9) beauty; (10) significance; (11) history.

[88] See account in Jou Chinqyun, *Bibliography of Chyn Books,* 3.9a–11a.

one printed in Yangjou in 1921 as a part of the compendium *Lianntyng Shyrell Joong* 棟亭十二種, the original texts of which were all owned by Tsaur Yin 曹寅 (1658–1712).

Chyn Shyy is first-hand material from the early Sonq period. It shows the Confucian scholar's outlook on music in general and the ideologies specifically connected with the *chyn*.[89] It is one of the earliest works emphasizing the type of people associated with the *chyn*. The author even went so far as to include sages and virtuous people who had no obvious connection with the instrument or even with music of any kind, but who had simply inspired certain *chyn* compositions.[90]

The book has been criticized because Ju seldom indicates fully his sources of information; and some of his quotations seem less complete than similar quotations made in other writings of later Sonq.[91] But he does include some useful details, for example, we also learn from him that in his own time the *chyn* was a popular instrument among the common people and that there were current at least two types of popular *chyn* music: the so-called *tsaunonq* 操弄, a purely instrumental type, notable for its ornamental figures; and music to accompany the so-called "vulgar" songs.[92]

Practical Treatises

The works to be discussed here deal largely with music for private performance rather than for official ceremonies and on the whole are more concerned with giving the literati useful information about the art than with ennobling his concept of its place in the cosmos—though they devote sufficient space to that, too. I shall examine here two major works and list a few instruction manuals for the *chyn* which although only partially preserved have proved to be helpful aids for transcribing the Sonq dynasty *chyn* tablature.

The *Tsyr Yuan* 詞源 [Sources of the *Tsyr*] deals with both the musical and textual composition of a special song form which reached the

---

[89] A portion of the *Chyn Shyy* (chap. 6) expounding his ideas has been translated by van Gulik, *The Chinese Lute*, pp. 54–55.

[90] For example, biographies of Chiu Yuan; Biann Her (chap. 2); An, the Prince of Hwainan; and Wang Jaujiun (chap. 3).

[91] A comparison between his biography of Tsuei Tzuenduh 崔遵度 (5. 2b–4b) and the biography of the same man in *Sonq History* is given in Jou Chinqyun's *Bibliography*, 3.3b–5b.

[92] 6.8a.

height of its development in the Sonq period. Its author, Jang Yan 張炎, was born in 1248 and died sometime after 1315.[93]

During the Yuan and Ming dynasties little was known of this work, and it was even confused with another book.[94] The earliest known printed version, from a Yuan manuscript,[95] was made in 1810 by Chyn Duenfuu 秦敦甫. During the nineteenth and the early twentieth centuries at least eight editions were issued, all stemming from the same Yuan manuscript.[96]

One needs only peruse the table of contents of Jang Yan's *Tsyr Yuan* to understand its importance. The work, in two main parts, contains thirty short sections. The beginning contains the ubiquitous diagrams and explanations of the tone system, the theoretical modes, and their cosmological significance. Following these are several topics of greater interest:

1) A concordance of the *liuhleu* and the *gongcheh* notations
2) The four notes in the higher octave
3) A concordance of the *gongcheh* notation and the popular notation of the Sonq period
4) A list of the nineteen modes actually in use during the Sonq period, with the notational symbols for the final of each mode

[93] The colophon to his book is by a Chyan Liangyow 錢良祐 who had met Jang Yan in 1315.

[94] Part of it was included in the supplement (*shiuhkan*) of a collection called *Baoyan tarng Mihjyi* 寶顏堂秘笈 brought together by Chern Jihru 陳繼儒 (1558–1639), where it was given the name *Yuehfuu Jyymi* 樂府指迷 (see *Syhkuh Weyshou Shumuh Tyiyaw* 四庫未收書目提要, 3.4a). The confusion existed as late as 1936, when it was perpetuated in H. J. Levis' *Foundations of Chinese Musical Art*, p. 216.

[95] *Guhgong Shannbeen Shumuh* [Catalogue of Rare Books in the Palace Museum], 1934, 3.22b, lists a facsimile of the Yuan manuscript copy.

[96] *Tsyrshyue Tsorngshu* edition, 1828, by Ge Day 戈載.
Shooushanger 守山閣 edition, 1843, by Chyan Shyijy 錢錫之, who collated the book with related materials in the Sonq History and in Jiang Kwei's *Baieshyr Dawren Gecheu*, which will be discussed later.
Yuehyeatarng 粤雅堂 edition, 1851–1862.
The *Tsyr Huah Tsorngkan* edition, 1853, by Wuu Chorngyaw 伍崇曜.
The *Yuyuan Tsorngke* 榆園叢刻 edition, 1893, by Sheu Tzeng 許增.
Tsyr Yuan, Peiping, 1925, edited by Wu Mei 吳梅.
Tsyr Yuan Jiaw Liuh 詞源斠律, a partially annotated edition by Jenq Wenjuo 鄭文焯 (1856–1918), in *Dahhehshanfarng Chyuanshu* 大鶴山房全書, vols. 1 and 2).
Tsyr Yuan Shujenq 詞源疏證, Nanking, 1932, punctuated and annotated by Tsay Jen 蔡楨. The editor bases many of his notes on *Tsyr Yuan Jiaw Liuh*, above, and the Sonq encyclopedia *Shyhlin Goangjih* (*SLGJ*; to be discussed later), but makes further collations with the above editions, and provides a facsimile of the original Yuan manuscript. This is now incorporated into the *Tsyr Huah Tsorngbian*, compiled by Tarng Gueijang 唐圭璋.

5) Rules for shifting from one mode to another in a single piece
6) Admonition on the correct intonation of the final note in a piece
7) A jingle on the secrets of how to sing properly.

These concordances of the different kinds of musical notation and the lists of modes in both the classical and popular nomenclature are keys to our understanding of Sonq musical theory and the deciphering of the Sonq popular notation.[97] In the second half of the book, among discussions of the literary craft of the *tsyr,* there are also short sections on the origins of the melodies, the various forms, and the total number and types of *pai* 拍 (beats?) used, a subject seldom found in works of previous periods. As a manual of *tsyr* composition for contemporary Sonq readers, the work took much for granted and is content with lists of terms where one would like explanation of procedures. Nevertheless, this is by far the most authoritative of the few known sources on *tsyr* of the Sonq period.

No other form of poetry in China since ancient times was so intimately related to music in the early stages of its development as was the *tsyr.*[98] It is believed that its verse patterns were evolved through the process of supplying words for existing melodies; hence the irregularity in the line length of the text. Gradually, while the *tsyr* became a literary genre (still practiced today by writers of verse in traditional forms), the music once associated with it was forgotten and the word patterns shaped by that music became merely literary models.

The period most productive of the *tsyr* was from the early tenth through the twelfth centuries. This treatise shows that in Jang Yan's day (late thirteenth century) the words and the music of the *tsyr* were still closely related, but to what extent and in what way the two elements affected each other in the creative process, is not made clear. Part of this answer, however, can be found in the musical examples in another Sonq dynasty work which we shall examine shortly.

The editing of Jang Yan's treatise has presented many problems. Scribes and wood-block cutters unfamiliar with the notational symbols inevitably distorted them in the process of copying and reprinting, and the technical terms in many cases have suffered a similar fate. Besides these mechanical difficulties, there are several passages, such as the

---

[97] The only other source useful for this purpose is the *SLGJ,* which came to the attention of modern scholars long after the *Tsyr Yuan* was known.

[98] Hightower, *Chinese Literature,* pp. 80–81; Glen W. Baxter, "Metrical Origins of the Tz'u, " *HJAS,* 16 (1953): 108–145.

instructions on proper singing techniques (I.61) and the section on the beats (II.14)[99] that are too cryptic to be understood fully by the modern reader. In spite of numerous collations and annotations by later scholars, many problems in Jang Yan's *Tsyr Yuan* must await further investigation.[100]

The second work containing information on music is the *Shyhlin Goang jih* 事林廣記 [A Comprehensive Record of the Forest of Affairs], an encyclopedia whose topics range from astronomy, geography, and biographies of famous men of ancient times, to sports, the art of cooking, and even a magic formula for winning at gambling.[101] It has several sections on music which are illustrated with charts, pictures, and musical examples.

The dates of the author, Chern Yuanjinq 陳元靚, are not certain. We know that he was active in the time of the Emperor Lii Tzong (r. 1225–1265) and received his *jinnshyh* degree (roughly comparable to the modern doctorate) in 1270.[102] The date of the first publication of this work is also unknown. The eight surviving copies of it are revised and enlarged. All editions have the basic title *Shyhlin Goang jih,* frequently modified as "illustrated," "supplemented," or "newly edited," and sometimes the book title is printed at the beginning of individual chapters in several variant forms.[103] The eight copies are located in the following places:

1) In the Library of the National Peking University, Peking, there is an edition of *Shyhlin Goang jih* in ten volumes, each divided into two chapters. The date is the sixth year of the Jyhyuan 至元 period of the Yuan dynasty. This is ambiguous because there happened to be two reigns during the Yuan that use this period title. The "sixth year of Jyhyuan" could be either 1269 or 1340. Both dates have been adopted in

---

[99] For a tentative interpretation of this passage see Wang Guangchyi, *History,* II.5.11.
[100] See Wu Mei's 吳梅 criticism in the preface of the Tsay Jen edition, p. 2.
[101] A very general description of this book appears in *Shiseki Kaidai* (An Annotated Bibliography of Historical Writings) by Endo Motō, *et al.* (Tokyo, 1940), p. 113.
[102] See *Syhkuh Tyiyaw,* II.1450.
[103] For example:
  1.7 纂圖增新群書類要事林廣記
  2 纂圖增類事林廣記
  3.5 新編纂圖增類群書類要事林廣記
  6.8 纂圖增新類聚事林廣記
As chapter headings there are:
  新編群書類要事林廣記
  新編分門事林廣記

[23]

Chinese bibliographies. [104]

2)   In the Archives and Mausolea Division (Shōryō-bu) of the Imperial Household Agency in Tokyo, there is a copy of *Shyhlin Goangjih*, the description of which corresponds to the edition mentioned above.[105] The date is given in the cyclical numbers, the *gengchern* 庚辰 year of the period of Jyhyuan. This is still ambiguous: it could be either 1280 or 1340.

3)   There is a privately owned Japanese collated edition printed in 1699 (preface dated 1684) which is based upon an edition of the Taydinq 泰定 period (1325).[106] It is in ten volumes, each subdivided into four to thirteen sections. It has some entries particularly useful to practicing musicians (see II. D.c, II.E, and II.G in listing below) that are not found in the other editions. Some of these extra passages are almost identical with sections of *Tsyr Yuan* (mentioned above) except that the sentences in the *SLGJ* are generally fuller.[107] Of all the editions it is most lacking in theoretical discussions (see I.A,B,C; II.D.a; Portion of III.A; III.G, below).

4)   In the Library of Jonggwo Keshyue Yuann (the Academia Sinica) in Peking, there is also a copy of the 1699 Japanese edition.[108]

5)   In the Palace Museum at Taiwan, there is a copy of *Shyhlin Goangjih* printed by the Chuenjuang Shuyuann 椿莊書院 in the reign of Jyhshuenn (1330–1333).[109] A considerable amount of new material has been added to this edition, and is indicated as such in the table of contents. The book is organized into forty-two chapters.

6)   In the Naikaku Bunko, a branch of the National Diet Library in

---

[104] In *Jonggwo Guuday Inyueh Shyyliaw Jyiyaw* 中國古代音樂史料輯要 [Selections of Ancient Chinese Musical Historical Sources], Peking, 1962, which reproduces the entire music sections of this work photographically (as supplement no. 1), the editors seem to favor the date 1340 (introduction, p. 6).

[105] See *Kunaishō Toshoryō kanseki zempon shomoku* [Catalogue of Chinese Rare Books in the Library of the Imperial Household Agency], 1929, 3.40.

[106] This edition has far fewer errors in the *chyn* tablature than the other editions. See also Yang Shooujinq 楊守敬 *Ryhbeen Faangshu Jyh* [Notes on a Bibliographic Tour of Japan], 1881, 11: 41–42, for appraisal of this edition. This also seems to be the edition cited by Wang Gwowei in his *History of Chinese Drama of the Sonq and Yuan Periods* (Shanghai, 1915). I am indebted to Dr. Herbert Franz Schurmann of the University of California at Berkeley for the loan of his personal copy. In subsequent discussions, unless otherwise specified, page references to *SLGJ* are to this Japanese edition.

[107] *SLGJ*, 5.61b, 65a; *Tsyr Yuan* 7.59.

[108] Included in the *Selections of Ancient Musical Sources* (see note 104) as supplement no. 2.

[109] See *Guhgong Shannbeen Shumuh* 2.9a–b. This is the chief edition used in the *Selections of Ancient Musical Sources*.

Tokyo,[110] there is a copy of *Shyhlin Goangjih* that seems to be printed from the same blocks as the Taiwan copy, except that the name of the printer's establishment is replaced by the words Shiyuan Jingsheh 西園精舍 cut in in an obviously different style. The contents in this copy are fuller.[111] The book, in fifty chapters, is grouped into four large sections.

There seems to be a curious relationship between the *chyn* section of edition numbers 5 and 6 and the *chyn* section of edition number 2. The tablatures from the two sources (III.E,F, below) are so similar in details (including even the mistakes) that they look as though printed from the same blocks. However, the alignment of the tablatures is different. Edition number 2 has eight units of symbols (each unit standing for either one note or a combination of two or three notes) to a column, while edition numbers 5 and 6 have seven. Considering the dates of these editions, and the fact that these units of symbols are widely spaced, it is conceivable that the same movable type was used and was arranged differently for the different printings.

7) There is in Seikadō Bunko, another branch of the National Diet Library in Tokyo, a 1418 edition of this work.[112] This is in six large divisions, each having two sections. The contents are almost the same as in edition number 6, but the order of some of the entries is changed. The calligraphy of the wood blocks in this edition is quite different from that in edition number 6, and, as we shall see later, some details from earlier editions are omitted.

8) In the Naikaku Bunko there is also a 1496 edition of the *Shyhlin Goangjih,* but this is simply a later printing from the blocks which were cut in 1418, with a minimum of emendations necessary for the occasion of the new printing.[113]

It seems, therefore, that there are basically only four different edi-

---

[110] See *Naikaku Bunko kanseki bunrui mokuroku* [Classified Catalogue of Chinese Books in the Naikaku Bunko], Tokyo, 1956, pp. 293–294. The edition in this library is now incomplete. Chaps. 5, 6, 7, and 8, which contain sections on music, are missing.

[111] See for example the passage after the modal concordance (II.D.b in the list of contents given below).

[112] This has the inscription: 永樂戊戌孟春翠巖精舍新刊 (Newly cut at the Tsueyyan Studio, in the first lunar month of the Wuhshiu year during the reign of Yeongleh). But at the end of the book there is also a colophon with the statement: 吳氏玉融書堂刊 (Cut at the Yuhrong Library of the Wu family).

[113] The inscription reads: 明弘治丙辰刊 (Cut in the Biingchern year during the reign of Horngjyh of the Ming dynasty). At the end of the book, there is also the statement: 詹氏進德書堂刊 (Cut at the Jinnder Library of the Jan family).

tions. Numbers 1 and 2 (which might be called the Jyhyuan edition, to retain the ambiguity of the dates); numbers 3 and 4 (the Japanese edition); numbers 5 and 6 (the Yuan edition); and numbers 7 and 8 (the Ming edition). In musical content, the main differences among the editions are:[114] the Jyhyuan edition does not have the seven melodies in the popular notation (IV.C in the listing below); the Japanese edition does not have the five *chyn* melodies (III.F). As for the other passages on musical matters, some have been added or omitted here and there; the order is sometimes a little different; and in some cases the same subject matter is presented in a different form. For example, the Jyhyuan and the Ming editions present the concordance of modal names in a large circular chart (II.D.a), while the Japanese and the Yuan editions have the concordance arranged in columns, to which is also added the scales of the modes in the popular notation (II.D.b). There are essentially four groups of entries dealing with music. A composite picture of these is presented in the following tabulation in which I give a description of the content under each heading rather than a translation of the title.[115]

Group I

A. Philosophical discussion of music
B. Illustrated description of twelve instruments for ceremonial music
C. Definitions of various musical terms
D. The origins of some ceremonial and popular instruments
E. Ancient ceremonial and popular dances

Group II

A. A circular diagram of the twelve semitones for the purpose of counting the sequence of fifths

[114] Among the eight editions, numbers 1 and 4 are not accessible to me.
[115] The titles read as follows:

Group I
A. 音樂總論
B. 樂器
C. 音樂名數
D. 音樂原始
E. 古代樂舞
Group II
A. 律呂隔八相生之圖
B. 四宮清聲
C. 律生八十四調
D. a. 五音律呂宮調之圖, b. 無名, c. 律呂宮商之圖, d. 無名
E. 宮調結聲正訛
F. 總叙訣, 八犯訣, 四犯訣, 寄煞訣
G. 管色指法

B. The four higher octave notes

C. A condensed chart of the eighty-four modes derived from the twelve pitches and the seven notes of the diatonic scale

D. Concordances of the classical and the popular modes[116]

    a. in a circular chart

    b. in vertical columns with scales written in the popular notation

    c. reduced circular chart with only 33 modes

    d. further reduced list of 19 modes which were currently in use

E. Corrections of some common mistakes in making cadences

F. Four rhymed instructions on how to compose a melody

G. Diagrams of various finger positions on the flute, each associated with one *gongcheh* and one popular notational symbol

Group III

A. General discussion of the *chyn*

B. Diagram of the instrument; woodcut of Confucius as a *chyn* player

C. Explanation of the symbols for the right-hand and left-hand techniques

D. Explanation of the reading of the tablature

E. Music with text *Kaijyy Hwanging Yn* 開指黃鶯吟 [An Introduction: "Song of the Golden Oriole"] written in tablature for the *chyn*

F. Five instrumental pieces for the *chyn* in tablature form, labeled by names that seem to suggest the mode:[117] "Gong Diaw" (fa), "Shang Diaw" (sol), "Jyue Diaw" (la), "Jyy Diaw" (do), "Yeu Diaw" (re)

G. Thirteen short lists of "do's" and "don'ts" regarding the playing

---

Group III
  A. 琴譜總説
  B. 琴圖,夫子杏壇之圖
  C. 右左手字譜
  D. 琴譜直解
  E. 開指黃鶯吟
  F. 五音調
  G. 調琴指要, 弾琴五功, 十善, 五能, 九不詳, 五病, 十疵, 五繆, 五不弾, 大病
      有七, 小病有五, 論十二病總括, 整琴要訣
Group IV
  A. 遏雲要訣
  B. 鼓板棒數
  C. 顧成雙等.

[116] See Chap. II, Table 2, for transcription in Western notation. This table has been discussed by Shiah Jinqguan in his *Tracing the Origins of Tsyr Tunes,* p. 21, where he also provides an equivalent list in the *gongcheh* notation.

[117] The actual music, however, shows that the prescriptions for these modes were not strictly followed. See notes to the transcriptions of these in Chap. IV.

and the care of the *chyn*

Group IV

A. Advice on singing by the Ehyun 遏雲 Society, with a sample of the text of a *juann* 賺 (a kind of medley)

B. Notation for a set of drum-beat patterns

C. A medley of seven melodies written in the Sonq popular notation:[118] *Yuann Cherng Shuang Linq* 願成雙令, *Yuann Cherng Shuang Mann* 願成雙慢, *Shytzyy Shiuh* 獅子序, *Beengong Poh Tzyy* 本宮破子, *Juann* 賺, *Shuangshenq Tzyy Jyi* 雙勝子急, *San Jiuh'erl* 三句兒

The constant reprinting and revising of *Shyhlin Goangjih* shows that it must have been a much-used handbook. In the musical field alone it is a remarkable work for many reasons. In the first place, there is a systematic nomenclature for popular modes. Further, though we are told that during Sonq in theory the basic scale (*gong-diaw*) from which all modes are derived is a fa scale, these examples show that a do scale was used as the *gong-diaw*.[119]

From the point of view of sources and notational systems, the *Shyhlin Goangjih* is important in having the third oldest example of *chyn* music found so far, and the second oldest existing in this tablature form,[120] some of whose symbols have archaic features no longer in use.[121] The seven textless melodies written in the popular notation are a substantial addition to the twenty extant Sonq dynasty examples using this notation.[122] These melodies are also significant for a different reason. Scholars of Sonq literature have long advanced the hypothesis that

[118] No. 5 is incomplete (see note 110, above), but these items are listed in the table of contents.

[119] Although the difference between the two scales is limited to only one note—the fourth degree of the fa scale being a semitone higher than the fourth degree of the do scale— the resulting melodies are quite different in style. There could have been a shift in this fourth degree during the late Sonq period (perhaps as a result of foreign influence), or quite possibly the two scales could have coexisted all along, since the *Swei History* (seventh Century) already mentions the existence of both types of scale. (See details on this point in Yang Inliou, *History*, p. 174.) As we shall see in Chap. III, the sets of symbols for the *gongcheh* and the popular notation of Sonq also suggest the existence of both scales.

[120] The two older examples are "Iou Lan" 幽蘭 (sixth century), which is simply a text explaining the execution of each single note, and "Guu Yuann" 古怨 by Jiang Kwei (1155–1221), which is in this tablature form but with no explanations. See further discussion of this system of notation in Chap. III.

[121] Wang Shyhshiang, "On the *Chyn* Melody *Goangling Sann*" (1959), p. 25.

[122] That is, the Seventeen *Tsyr* Songs by Jiang Kwei and the three short pieces presented in the Ming work *Cheu Liuh*, both to be discussed later.

poetic texts were written to existing melodies, and these are the only examples of such stock melodies.

Finally, besides these pieces of actual music, we find in *Shyhlin Goangjih* the unusual diagrams of flute fingering with covered and uncovered holes with their related notational symbols, making explicit an affinity of the popular notation with this instrument which has so far only been surmised.[123]

Portions of many Sonq manuals on *chyn* playing which no longer exist independently have been incorporated into later books such as the *Yeongleh Chyn Shu Jyicherng* 永樂琴書集成 [Comprehensive Collection of Treatises on the *Chyn* from the Yeongleh Reign], which dates from some time before 1425,[124] and the *Tayguu Yi In* 太古遺音 (Sounds from the Past), by the Ming prince Ju Chyuan 朱權 in 1413.[125] Although fragmentary, these manuals are useful in explaining the meaning of some tablature symbols that do not appear in *chyn* music of later times.[126] Quotations from these manuals are usually clearly indicated as such in the compilations. However, since we have no idea of the editions of the Sonq manuals at the time they were drawn on by the compilers, who lived over two hundred years later, caution is necessary in using them as authentic Sonq sources.[127]

Notes on Music in Sonq Memoirs and Collected Works

The three works discussed in this section are memoirs or miscellaneous writings of Sonq authors which contain important passages on

[123] Yang Yinnliou has corrected a few mistakes in the diagrams. See his *Studies of the Songs Composed by Jiang Bairshyr of the Sonq Dynasty* (Peking, 1957), p. 15.

[124] This work, compiled upon imperial order, is the most comprehensive Ming compilation on the *chyn*. The original manuscript is now in the Palace Museum in Taipei. A printed copy was made in 1590 by Jeang Kehchian 蔣克謙, who added two chapters containing music and changed the title to *Chyn Shu Dahchyuan* 琴書大全; a manuscript copy of this printed edition is now preserved at the Institute of Ethnomusicology in Peking. See Uang Menqshu 汪孟舒 "Annotations to the *Usylan* Manual" (mimeographed copy, Peking, 1955), p. 29a-b; and Ja Fuhshi, *Bibliography*, I.22b.

[125] Annotated by Yuan Jiunjer 袁均哲 between 1436 and 1450. See Uang Menqshu, p. 28a-b, in which the contents of the available early sources on the *chyn* are systematically presented.

[126] The following are the original titles of some of these manuals: *Tayguu Yi In Jyi* 太古遺音集 by Tyan Jy'ueng 田之翁; *Jyetzow Jyyfaa* 節奏指法 by the Monk, Tzer Chyuan 則全; *Mingshuh Faduan* 名數發端 by Cherng Yuhjiann 成玉磵; *Chyn Yuan Shiu Jy* 琴苑須知 by Yang Tzuuyun 楊祖雲; *Ju Jia Jyyfaa Shyr Yi* 諸家指法拾遺, anonymous; *Tarn Chyn Shooushyh Twu* 弹琴手勢圖, anonymous (see Uang, *Usylan*, p. 27).

[127] Uang, *Usylan*, p. 27.

music. We deal here not with systematic discussions or accounts but with incidental references to musical matters in books of more general interest. In most cases the musical topic occupies no more than a paragraph. Nevertheless, these passages are by writers who were quite competent on the subject, and what they noted often has much practical value.

The only work in this group that belongs to the Northern Sonq period is the *Menqshi Biitarn* 夢溪筆談 or *Memoirs from Menqshi* by Sheen Gua 沈括 (1031–1095).[128] The author was an unusually versatile scholar with a lively interest in science and technology as well as in social and artistic activities, and he had a keen interest both in his own times and in historical topics. He wrote the *Memoirs* sometime after 1086, and it was published soon after. The original book was divided into twenty-six chapters, each with fifteen to thirty entries. Three chapters of *Additional Memoirs* (*Buu Biitarn*) and one chapter of *Further Memoirs* (*Shiuh Biitarn*) were published posthumously. Today there exist no less than nine editions of the *Memoirs* printed between 1495 and 1934, all based directly or indirectly on an edition of 1166.[129]

The musical entries are found in chapters 5 (paragraphs 82–110)[130] and 6 (paragraphs 111–115) and in chapter 1 (paragraphs 530–541) of the *Additional Memoirs*. Sheen Gua begins with discussions of ritual music and the pitches, which occupy the first four paragraphs. These are followed by a long series of entries (paragraphs 86–110) on a great variety of subjects. Most of them concern popular music: for example, per-

---

[128] For a general account of this work and a list of its contents by categories, see Joesph A. Needham, *Science and Civilization in China* (Cambridge, Eng., 1954), I, 135–137. Needham renders the title as "Dream Pool Essays."

[129] Some of these include the supplements, others do not. In 1956 *A Critical Edition of Menqshi Memoirs,* was published in Shanghai by Hwu Dawjinq 胡道靜, who collated all the existing editions, brought together annotations on the work by numerous scholars, and added notes of his own. In the preface of this edition, Hwu also gives a detailed account of the various printings of the *Menqshi Memoirs* and its supplements, with photographic samples of all editions now extant. All editions of the *Memoirs* have mistakes in the passages containing musical notation. Even Hwu in his collated edition often prefers the wrong reading (which is printed in the regular-size type of the text, but at least he preserved the other readings). Some of the more serious mistakes (see also Kishibe, "Twenty-eight Modes," p. 459) are:
Paragraph 531, line 2: for *shanq* 上 read *gou* 勾.
Paragraph 541, line 4: for *shanq* 上 read *gong* 工.
Paragraph 541, line 12: for *syh* 四 read *gong* 工.
Paragraph 541, line 14: for *cheh* 尺 read *gou* 勾.

[130] Paragraph references are to Hwu's convenient modern edition.

formances on a special kind of drum; the construction of the zither and the flute; division of musical sections; the origins of some well-known pieces; the problems of diction in singing; the origin of the *tsyr* songs; a study of some ancient bells discovered in the author's time; and so forth. In chapter 6 (paragraphs 111–115) Sheen Gua concentrates mostly on the problems of pitch in popular music. The twelve entries in the *Additional Memoirs* are supplementary discussions of some of the topics dealt with earlier. Here Sheen Gua defines the popular modes in greater detail, adding comments on an unusual method of tuning the zither, problems of pitches in certain bells and chimes, and so forth.

As pointed out by Joseph Needham,[131] Sheen Gua is perhaps the most interesting figure in all Chinese scientific history. In musical matters he makes critical remarks on the mystical treatment of a mathematical passage in the *Hann History's* "Monograph on Measurement and Calculation" which is, in fact, no more than some calculations on the length of pitch pipes (paragraph 85); he argues that old chimes cannot retain their original pitches after polishing (paragraph 97); and he explains the phenomenon of resonant strings, which bewildered the owner of a seemingly enchanted lute (paragraph 115).

In factual details Sheen Gua provides information on several musical forms, such as the *tsyr* songs (paragraph 95), the *Kaege* 凱歌 or "triumphant songs" (paragraph 90), and the *dahcheu* 大曲 or suite (paragraph 88). However, more important are his entries on the music system of the Northern Sonq which include description of the popular modes and their cadencing notes (paragraph 531, 541, to be discussed in Chapter II). On these matters Sheen Gua is much more precise than the author of the official treatise *Jiingyow Yueh Swei Shin Jing*,[132] the only other Northern Sonq source on the popular modes. It is significant that in certain details the two sources differ.[133]

Sheen Gua's description of the modes in paragraph 114 is well known as the earliest documentation for the use of *gongcheh* symbols in Chinese sources.[134] His description by means of musical notation clarifies considerably the confusion in the study of the popular modal systems of the Northern and Southern Sonq periods, a problem which seems to lie

[131] Needham, *Science and Civilization*, p. 135. See also the more recent study by Donald Holzman, "Shen Kua and His *Meng-ch'i pi-t'an*," in *T'oung Pao*, 46 (1958): 260–292. However, Holzman is not concerned with Sheen's musical writings.

[132] 景祐樂髓新經. See above, p. 15.

[133] See p. 51.

[134] See also Wang Guangchyi, *History*, II.7.

more in the terminologies of the modes than in the modes themselves. The modes given by Sheen Gua are basically similar to those in *Shyhlin Goangjin* of the Southern Sonq,[135] but Sheen's description is fuller and actually fits better the musical examples of the Southern Sonq, as we shall see in the discussion on modes in Chapter III.

I have mentioned before in the section on theoretical treatises Ju Shi's interest in music as a part of the Confucian way of life. Besides his annotations on classical writings about music (see above), he also wrote many short notes about other aspects of music which are scattered through his collected works.[136] The most important of these is the series of remarks on the *chyn* under the title "Chyn Liuh Shuo" 琴律説 (Discourses on the Pitches of the *Chyn*), in his *Ju Tzyy Dahchyuan* 朱子大全 (The Collected Works of the Philosopher Ju), which is preserved today in Sonq and later editions.[137]

In these notes Ju Shi describes the fret positions of the *chyn*, the pitches, and the basic tuning system. It was not his intention to give mere factual information or to instruct players; he was trying to justify, in terms of Confucian metaphysics, the numerical relationships which he had found in the measurements of the instument. Of more interest to music historians are his criticisms, for example, of the arbitrary manner in which musicians decided on the pitches for stringed instruments. It is in an attempt to make his thesis clear to all that Ju Shi includes a list of the symbols of the popular notation with their equivalents expressed in the *liuhleu* and *gongcheh* notations, a list which became known as the earliest source on the Sonq popular notation.[138]

[135] Some similarities in these two sources have been mentioned by Shiah Jinqguan, *Tracing the Origins of Tsyr Tunes*, pp. 23–25.

[136] Another collection of Ju Shi's works that also contains some occasional notes on music is his *Collected Discourses*.

[137] The collection, in one hundred chapters, is traditionally said to have been compiled by the master's son, Ju Tzay 朱在. Two supplements, in ten and twenty chapters respectively, were added later by other Sonq scholars. At least two editions from the Sonq period are extant today, one dated 1265 and the other, with the supplements, undated; the undated edition has been partially reprinted with Ming restorations. A copy is now in the National Central Library at Taipei. See Chang Biider's *Catalogue*, p. 27. There are many other Ming and Ching editions. Currently available editions are the *Syhbuh Tsorngkan* edition of 1929 which is a photolithograph of a Jiajinq (嘉靖 1522–1566) edition, the *Syhbuh Beyyaw* edition of 1927 (based on that of 1532), and an 1810 edition printed by Shyu Shuhming 徐樹銘. But the order of contents of the Shyu Shuhming edition is quite different from that of the 1532 edition, and it contains two extra characters (兀 and 五, p. 36a, line 2) in his comment on the popular notation of the Sonq dynasty.

[138] The other sources are in Jiang Kwei's songs (see below) and *SLGS*, both differing from this list in a few details.

The *Bihji Mannjyh* 碧鶏漫志 [Random Notes from Bihji] by Wang Jwo 王灼 (fl. 1160) is a work mainly of literary interest. It is relevant to the present inquiry because the genre with which it principally deals is the *tsyr* lyric which, as we have seen, is closely related to music. It survives now in several Ming and Ching editions.[139]

This book, in five chapters, begins with general comments on songs, singing, and singers. In the last three chapters where Wang Jwo deals specifically with twenty-eight well-known pieces of music (to which many different lyrics were fitted), he gives accounts of their origin, their variant titles, and in many instances a description of their formal structure. In describing many pieces, such as "Nicharng Yeu'i Cheu" 霓裳羽衣曲, "Ijou" 伊州, and "Luh'iau" 六么, Wang Jwo draws from Tarng sources. His comparisons of new and old versions of some of the songs show changes in their form and mode, and in his comments on the general musical practices of his time, he records concordances of the popular and classical names of modes, gives the names of the standard movements of the *dahcheu*, comments on the use of a mode throughout such a suite like structure, and cites in the *gongcheh* notation the irregular cadencing in certain modes.

Song Collections with Notes and Comments

In this section I shall deal with two song collections. Since the music itself will be transcribed and discussed in the following chapter, only a general description and bibliographical information of these works will be given here.

The *Bairshyr Dawren Gecheu* 白石道人歌曲 [Songs of Whitestone, the Taoist] is the most famous of all musical sources from the Sonq dynasty. The man who called himself Whitestone the Taoist was the well-known Southern Sonq poet Jiang Kwei 姜夔 (1155–1221).[140] This collection contains Jiang Kwei's poems, twenty-eight of which have musical settings, twenty-three composed by the poet himself.

The earliest printing of the *Songs of Whitestone,* according to the

[139] The two Ming editions (*Shuo Fwu* and *Tarng Sonq Tsorngshu* editions) have no prefaces and the texts are incomplete. Only in the *Jybutzwujai* 知不足齋 printing of 1884 do we find a presumably complete text with the author's preface. This is a collated edition based upon another Ming copy (*Jiguuger edition*) and from it another reprint, in the *Tsyr Huah Tsorngbian,* was made in 1935.

[140] See Yang Yinnliou's *Studies,* pp. 8–11; Shiah Cherngtaur, *Biographies of Tsyr Poets of the Tarng and Sonq Dynasties* (Shanghai, 1955), pp. 425–445.

colophon, was made by one Chyan Shiwuu 錢希武 in the year 1202, when Jiang Kwei was in his forties. Unfortunately this edition is no longer extant. Other early printings, especially from the Ming period, are often incomplete, omitting the musical notations.[141] There is, however, a full manuscript copy made in 1350 by the Yuan scholar Taur Tzongyi 陶宗儀, and a later collation made by the same scholar in 1360 from what he describes as a better copy. Two printings are derived from the 1360 collation, one by Luh Jonghuei 陸鍾輝 in 1743 and one by Jang Yihshu 張奕樞 in 1749. Both editions are rare today, but the Luh edition has been photolithographically reproduced (1929) for the *Syhbuh Tsorngkan* series. These two editions which have served as the basis for several later editions.[142] are in most cases regrouped into four chapters.

Although the Luh and Jang editions were based on the same manuscript and printed only a few years apart, numerous discrepancies have been found between them.[143] There is a third copy made from the Yuan manuscript by Jiang Biingnan 江炳南 in 1737 which, however, was not printed until 1913.[144] As it has preserved the original format of six chapters, I have used it in making the following outline of those contents related to music.[145]

Chapter 1. The song "Guu Yuann" 古怨 [Old Regrets] with chyn accompaniment written in tablature with preliminary discussion of the mode and the specific tuning for the piece.

Chapter 2. "Yueh Jeouge" 越九歌 (Ritual Songs for Yueh),[146] a group of ten songs with music in the *liuhleu* notation (numbered I to X in the following discussion). A concordance of the *liuhleu* notation with the

[141] For example, the *Jyiguuger* edition (Seventeenth century) and the *Chindinq Tsyr Puu* 欽定詞譜 version (1715). An account of some unsatisfactory editions is given by Jiang Biingnan 江丙南 in his preface to the *Chyangtsuen Tsorngshu* 彊村叢書 (a large repository of *tsyr* poetry printed in the 1913 edition discussed below in this chapter.

[142] For example, the *Yuyuan Tsorngke* 榆園叢刻 edition (ed. Sheu Tzeng, 1893), *Syhbuh Beyyaw* (1934), and the *Tsorngshu Jyicherng* edition (1939). Chiou Chyongsuen, in his *Bairshyr Dawren Gecheu Tongkao* [Comprehensive Investigation of the Songs of Whitestone the Taoist], has listed thirty-eight known editions.

[143] Jang Wenhuu 張文虎 in 1862 made a collation of the two editions.

[144] In *Chyangtsuen Tsorngshu* (see note 141).

[145] Actually the order of appearance of the pieces in both versions is exactly the same except that in the Luh and Jang editions the songs in chapter 2 are placed before "Guu Yuann" in chapter 1.

[146] The title literally means "The Nine Songs of Yueh." It is an allusion to the "Jeouge" (Nine Hymns) in the *Song of the South*. See also Laurence Picken, "Chiang K'ui's Nine Songs for Yueh," pp. 201–202.

gongcheh notation. An explanation of the technique of *jer-tzyh* 折字 presumably calling for a kind of microtonal shading.

Chapter 3: Four *linq* 令 songs[147] with musical settings in the popular notation: (1) "Lihshimei Linq" 鬲溪梅令. (2) "Shinqhuatian" 杏花天. (3) "Tzueyynshang Sheaupiin" 醉吟商小品. (4) "Yuhmei Linq" 玉梅令.

Chapter 4: One *mann* 慢 song with musical setting in the popular notation: (5) "Nicharng Jongshiuh Dih'i" 霓裳中序第一.

Chapter 5: Nine songs by Jiang Kwei[148] with musical settings in the popular notation: (6) "Yangjou Mann" 揚州慢. (7) "Charngtyngyuann Mann" 長亭怨慢. (8) "Dannhwangleou" 淡黃柳. (9) "Shyrhwushian" 石湖仙. (10) "Annshiang" 暗香. (11) "Shuyiing" 疏影. (12) "Shihorng'i" 惜紅衣. (13) "Jyueshaur" 角招. (14) "Jyyshaur" 徵招.

Chapter 6: Three songs composed by Jiang Kwei[149] written in the popular notation: (15) "Chioushiau Yn" 秋霄吟. (16) "Chiliang Fann" 凄涼犯. (17) "Tsueylou Yn" 翠樓吟.

The music of Number 1 and Number 2 are by unknown composers. Number 3, according to Jiang Kwei in his preface to the song, he learned from a *pyiba* player who gave him the melody in *pyiba* tablature. Number 4 was composed by the contemporary poet Fann Cherngdah 范成大 originally without a text. As for Number 5, Jiang says in his note that it was one of eighteen textless melodies that he found among a pile of old books belonging to some musicians in Charngsha and which, in his opinion, were different in style from the current music of his time.

The preservation of the *Songs of Whitestone the Taoist* probably owes more to the words than to the music. Certainly to some of the Ming editors, who went so far as to omit the music altogether, Jiang Kwei was more appreciated as a poet. Only in the early eighteenth century, when the Yuan manuscript copy was found and printed, was the book generally recognized as a precious source for the study of Chinese music of the past.

From the earliest attempt in 1777 to decipher the popular notation in this book to the most recent studies in 1959, no less than fifteen authors

---

[147] The Sonq sources are frustratingly vague in definition of the terms *linq* 令, *mann* 慢, *yiin* 引, and so forth, but the contexts (for example, Jang Yan's *Tsyr Yuan*, II. 6–7, 48) suggest that they denote formal characteristics. See also Shiah Jinqguan, *Origins of Tsyr Tunes*, pp. 48–54, and remarks in Chap. IV.

[148] This group is called "tzyh duh cheu" 自度曲 (melodies composed by himself).

[149] This section is called "tzyh jyh cheu" 自製曲 . Jiang Kwei seems to use this and "tzyh duh cheu" interchangeably in his book.

have written books or articles on various aspects of Jiang Kwei's music.[150] Through study of the Sonq theoretical works on music (such as Jang Yan's *Tsyr Yuan* and the music sections of *Shyhlin Goangjih,* both of which came to light only after Jiang Kwei's songs were rediscovered), the basic problems of reading the music can be solved.

These songs by Jiang Kwei, with both the text and music preserved, reveal some interesting principles behind musical composition of his time. Table 1 shows the relationship in melodic material among the *tsyr* songs and between the *tsyr* and his ritual songs for Yueh (On the names of the modes, *fa* of *c,* and so forth, see Chapter II.)

The most closely related pairs are 6 and 7, 10 and 11, 13 and 14, V and 12, X and 1, VI and 17, which although containing variations are obviously the same melodies. Other groups such as 9 and 15 and 17, III and 2, VIII and 4, and so forth, have occasional common phrases which sometimes appear in a different order. It is a method of composing that still exists in present-day Chinese musical drama and also in many ways resembles the use of type melodies or patchwork melodies in the medieval Gregorian chant.[151]

The two-stanza form of the text in these *tsyr* songs (usually with a slight variation in the second stanza) and the syllabic style of the musical setting make it easy to observe in detail Jiang Kwei's procedure in text setting. Here, one finds that music was adjusted to the form of the text to the extent that at times no consideration seems to be given to the phrasing of the melody.[152] One can conclude that in Jiang Kwei's *tsyr*

---

[150] Shiah Cherngtaur (Bibl. no. 76, pp. 2559–2588) in 1932 gave a detailed descriptive list, with critical comments, of many early efforts, and in 1956 (Bibl. no. 79) a categorized and more up-to-date list. It may, however, be useful to give here a list of the more important studies on these problems, with reference to the bibliography at the end of this book. Studies attempting to identify the symbols of the popular notation in meaningful musical terms include Bibliography items nos. 44, 48, 49, 67, 75, 83, and 95. (For a controversy over the origin of the popular notation, see no. 60). Studies providing special collation of the different editions of the *tsyr* songs include Bibliography nos. 57 and 77. On Jiang Kwei's own musical annotations see no. 79 (pp. 145–175). Transcriptions are found in the following sources. The Ritual Songs for Yueh: Bibliography nos. 48 (1833), 44 (1858), 81 (1931), 63 (1936), 69 (1957), 95 (1957). "Guu Yuann": nos. 48 (1833), 50 (1924), 70 (1957), 71 (1966), 95 (1957). The Seventeen *Tsyr* Songs: nos. 48 (1833), 83 (1931), 46 (1942), 79 (1956), 95 (1957), 85 (1958), 45 (1959).

[151] See, for example, *The New Oxford History of Music,* II, 110. Picken notices this practice also in the ritual melodies cited by Ju Shi (Picken, *Twelve Ritual Melodies,* pp. 168–169).

[152] See for example the last lines of the two stanzas in song No. 10; and also the first lines of No. 17 in Chap. IV.

Table 1. Relationship between the ritual songs for Yueh and the Seventeen *Tsyr* Songs

Ritual songs (in Roman numerals)	*Tsyr* songs (in Arabic numerals)
fa-modes	
I: fa of c	
II: fa of e-flat, some suggestion of 6, 7	6: fa of e-flat; 7: fa of e-flat, same material as 6
V: fa of b-flat, same material as 12	12: fa of b-flat
	10: fa of a-flat; 11: fa of a-flat, same material as 10
re-modes	
X: re of d-flat, same material as 1 moved a 4th above	
	8: re of f
VIII: re of g, suggestion of 4	4: re of g
VII: re of a-flat	1: re of a-flat; 16: re of a-flat, suggestion of 10, 11!
sol-modes	
IV: sol of c	
VI: sol of e-flat, same material as 17	3: sol of e-flat; 17: sol of e-flat, some lines in common with 9 at different pitches
	5: sol of a-flat
IX: sol of a, not a regular Sonq mode	
III: sol of b-flat, suggestion of 2, 9, 15	2, 9, 15: all sol of b-flat, 9 and 15 have many common materials
	13: la of c, not a regular Sonq mode
	14: do of c, not a regular Sonq mode; same material as 13

songs music was the pre-existing element and that it was flexible; whereas the text, whose form may have been only created for this song, was the less compromising partner in its union with music.

The identity of these musical types is another interesting point. It is not, as one might expect, in the so-called "tune titles" of a given *tsyr* song. (These tune titles later became labels for their verse forms.) Table 1 shows that songs with the same musical materials, whole or fragmentary, are, in most cases, in the same mode. The same is true of the two pairs X and 1, and 17 and 9 which are in different scales but are both re modes and sol modes respectively. The relationship between 16 and 10 and 11 is an exception which will be discussed later.[153] Although these examples are rather limited, they are sufficient to prove that the modal theory during this period was closely related to the identification of melody types.[154]

Jiang Kwei is one of the few known composers of the Sonq period.[155] His fondness for experimenting with theoretical modes and his interest in recovering old forgotten music show that his approach to music was an intellectual one. He was also interested in court music and in 1179 presented a book on methods of revising the court music, *Dahyueh Yih* 大樂議 [Expounding the Great Music],[156] which, however, was not adopted by the authorities.

Other interesting musical features of Jiang Kwei's songs are closely related to notational problems and will be discussed in Chapter III.

The second musical collection, preserved only in a very small fragment, is a Ming citation from a Sonq collection of music. It is variously called *Yuehfuu Dahchyuan* 樂府大全, *Yuehfuu Hwencherng* 樂府渾成, or simply *Huenncherngjyi* 混 [*sic*] 成集.[157] The reference is in a treatise by Wang Jihder 王驥德 called *Cheu Liuh* 曲律 [Music of the *Cheu* Songs] (*cheu* being successors to the *tsyr*), the preface of which is dated 1610.[158] Wang Jihder cites from the old book three short pieces of music which use the same popular notation used by Jiang Kwei.[159] He gives the following account of how he came across them:[160]

[153] See notes to the transcription of No. 16 in Chap. IV.

[154] Again this is not unique in the Far East. See *The New Oxford History of Music*, II, 42–43.

[155] The other two are Shyong Pernglai (*Seh Puu*) and Fann Cherngdah (composer of melody No. 4).

[156] The work, no longer extant, is quoted in *Sonq History*, 4821c-d.

[157] The term *yuehfuu*, originally applied to the Music Bureau which collected popular songs in the Hann dynasty, came to refer to the songs themselves and eventually, in loose usage, to songs of all periods, as here. The three titles may be roughly rendered Compendium of Songs, Potpourri of Songs, and Potpourri Collection.

[158] First printed by Wang Jihder's pupil, Mau Yiisuey 毛以燧 (Colophon 1624, preface by Ferng Menqlong 馮夢龍, 1625). The Ming edition in the Palace Museum in Taiwan is presumably the original. In 1842 it was reprinted in *Jyy Hae* (photolithographed in 1936) and also served as the basis for the *Shyueshuh Tsorngbian* 學術叢編 (1916) and the *Sonqfenshyh Tsorngshu* 誦芬室叢書 (1922).

[159] See *Jyy Hae* edition, 4.39, "Miscellaneous Notes," 2.2b-3g. The three pieces should really, perhaps, be considered as two pieces with a short introduction (see notes to my transcription in Chap. IV).

[160] Page 1b.

When I was in the capital a friend one day brought to show me a printed volume from the *Yuehfuu Dahchyuan*, also called *Yuehfuu Hwencherng*, which had been kept in the Imperial Library [the Wen'iuanger 文淵閣]. This is a collection of the *tsyr* of Sonq and Yuan times—that is [the interpolation is Wang's] *cheu*-songs. In the category of the *Linjong-shang* 林鐘商 mode alone there are over two hundred pieces of *tsyr*, none of which I had ever seen before in my life. Judging from the other possible categories of modes, there must have been a great deal more to this work; the total should be several dozen volumes. The contents listed here are names of pieces no longer extant. The notation depicted here is entirely different from that of present day musicians . . . From this we know that books of *tsyr* and *cheu* originally must have been numerous. Even of the *cheu* current today there must be many comprehensive collections. It would be regrettable if they should become scattered and their tradition lost. In the following I shall list the table of contents and copy down the musical notation to preserve an example of what the entire work is like.

In the table as recorded by Wang Jihder the heading is the classical modal name *Linjong-shang*, and this is followed by the phrase "called *Shiejyydiaw* 歇指調 during the Swei dynasty" (590–619). Nineteen compositions in this mode are listed,[161] of which the first two are described by the same names as the music given to illustrate them.

The first piece, with the heading "Shiausheng Puu" 娟聲譜 [Music of Introduction (?)], has no text. It is simply a five-note phrase that spells the scale of the mode. The second piece, with the heading "Sheaupiin Puu" 小品譜 (Music of a Little Piece), has nineteen notes with text; and the third, simply labeled *yow* 又 [Another Example], has twenty-one notes with text.[162]

In searching for earlier references to the *Yuehfuu Dahchyuan*, I found none (under any of its names) in any of the standard bibliographies in the great compendia of or for the Sonq Dynasty, nor in the better known catalogues of private libraries of the period. There is, however, an account of this collection in the memoirs of the poet Jou Mih 周密 (1232–1308). According to his *Chyidong Yeeyeu* 齊東野語 [Words of a

---

[161] As follows: (1) 娟聲, (2) 品 (有大品小品), (3) 歌曲子, (4) 唱歌, (5) 中腔, (6) 踏歌, (7) 引, (8) 三臺, (9) 傾盃樂, (10) 慢曲子, (11) 促拍, (12) 令, (13) 序, (14) 破子, (15) 急曲子, (16) 木笪, (17) 丁聲長行, (18) 大曲, and (19) 曲破. Note that the second title in the table of contents is simply *piin*, with a note, "there are big *piin* and little *piin*."

[162] Transcription of this group of pieces has been attempted by Tarng Lan, "A Study of the Side Notation in the Songs of Whitestone the Taoist," in *Dongfang Tzarjyh*, 1931, p. 70.

Fool from Chyidong],[163] "*Huenncherngjyi* 混成集 was printed by the Bureau of Reparation of the Palace and the Temple of the Royal Ancestors.[164] There are more than a hundred large volumes, comprising the most complete collection of the music of old and new *tsyr*. In the category of the *dahcheu* alone there is a total of several hundred stanzas,[165] and so one can imagine the rest. However, about one-half of this has only music and no text."

The compilation seems to date from the very late Sonq or early Yuan period. At least one eminent bibliographer has assigned it to the latter.[166] There appears to be no surviving mention of it from Yuan times, however. Assuming the information of its discoverer, Wang Jihder, to be correct, by early Ming there was or had been a set in the Imperial Library, though the fifteenth-century catalogue of the library does not include it.[167] In a smaller and much later catalogue of the same library, *Catalogue of Books Preserved in the Cabinet Library* of 1605,[168] there is the following entry: "*Yuehfuu Hwencherngjyi*—105 volumes (incomplete). The compiler's name is unknown. It consists entirely of *tsyr* and includes music notation. The arrangement is by categories in terms of the five notes of the scale and the twelve pitches.[169] Originally there were 127 volumes; 22 are now missing." It may be that Wang Jihder's citation of the musical examples was from one of the 22 missing volumes.

By the end of the Ming dynasty many of the works in the Imperial Library were partially or wholly lost, and the larger part of those then remaining disappeared early in the Ching period.[170] The last appearance

---

[163] *Shyuejin Taoyuan* ed., 10.17a, line 1.

[164] The Shiouneysy 修內司.

[165] Tentatively rendering *jiee* 解 as "stanza." It is different from a "section" of a suite, for which the author uses the term *duann* 段 as later in the same paragraph (霓裳一曲共三十段).

[166] Hwang Yujyi; see below, p. 41.

[167] *Wen'iuanger Shumuh* 文淵閣書目 (1441) by Yang Shyhchyi 楊士奇, *et al*. The omission may simply be an error, since this catalogue is poorly organized. The musical entries, for instance, are scattered in three different places—with the Classics, poetry and poetics, and art books. See also Teng and Biggerstaff, *Annotated Bibliography*, p. 22.

[168] By Suen Cherngchwan 孫成傳, *et al*. MS copy in the Chinese-Japanese Library at Harvard. (See also Teng and Biggerstaff, p. 23). The quotation is from 5. 1b–2a, Section on Music 樂律部.

[169] That is, the names of the classical modes, see Chap. II.

[170] Teng and Biggerstaff, p. 22. The authors further tell us that 20,000 volumes were rediscovered in the Archievs of the Grand Secretariat in 1909. In 1933 the Institute of History and Philology of Academia Sinica (Peiping) published an edited and printed copy of a series of 20 catalogues which are found in the Archives. Some musical books are included in the lists, but *Yuehfuu Hwencherng* is not there.

of the name *Yuehfuu Hwencherng* seems to be in *Chianchiing Tarng Shumuh*[171] 千頃堂書目, the catalogue of the personal library of the great bibliophile Hwang Yujyi 黄虞稷 (1629–1691). Hwang simply gives the title, notes that there are 105 volumes, and includes it with other books from the Yuan dynasty.[172]

Materials on the Social Background of Sonq Music

Several works written during and shortly after the Sonq dynasty describe the city life of its northern and southern capitals, Kaifeng and Hangchow. They are sketches rather than sociological studies, but they contain detailed descriptions of many of the social conventions of the time—for example, the ways in which people celebrated holidays, festivals, weddings, and birthdays. There are also listings of different kinds of shops, restaurants, houses of entertainment; of foods, clothing, utensils; and of people (often by name) in various occupations, including even certain types of hoodlums and loafers. The authors wrote with nostalgia, at a time when the country was already partially conquered by aliens or when the Sonq dynasty had been swept away completely. To these writers nothing was either too general or too trivial for them to record.

Music played an important part in the life of the Sonq cities. We find in these books not only names of musical instruments and of performers but descriptions of a great variety of songs, dances, and theater music. There are records of the make-up of an entire orchestra and the musical programs of royal festivities.

It is impossible to make a complete list of all the books that contain occasional mention of musical matters in Sonq times. I shall list only a few of the most significant works.

Dong jing Meng Hwa Luh 東京夢華錄 (1147), by Menq Yuanlao 孟元老, in ten chapters, covers the period 1102–1125. The outstanding passages are those on street entertainers (chapter 5, pages 29–30),[173] on court festivals (chapter 9, page 52), and on a sacrificial ceremony (chapter 10, page 59). This work, incidentally, is extensively quoted in *Shyhlin Goangjih* for its information about institutional matters.

---

[171] See Teng and Biggerstaff, p. 25, or for a detailed description of this personal library, see 錢謙益, 牧齋有樂記 (26. 3a–4b).

[172] 32. 24b. This bibliography is the source from which Chyan Dahshin 銭大昕, in 1800, reconstructed the bibliographical monograph for the official *New Yuan History*, in which *Yuehfuu Hwencherng Jyi* is included. See 八史經籍志, 14.4.27b.

[173] The pagination followed here is that of the Shanghai edition of 1956 (see note 185).

Ducherng Jih Shenq 都城紀勝 (1235), by Nay Derueng 耐得翁, in one chapter, covers the entire period of the Southern Sonq dynasty. The outstanding feature of this book is a section containing the most complete description we have of the formal structure of the type of medley called *juann* 賺 (page 98).

Menq Liang Luh 夢粱録 (ca. 1275), by Wu Tzyhmuh 吳自牧, in twenty chapters, is a large work dealing mostly with the Southern Sonq capital. Its musical sections include a good many borrowings from the two books described above,[174] but its accounts are slightly fuller.

Wuulin Jiowshyh 武林舊事 (between 1280 and 1290), by Jou Mih 周密, in ten chapters, is notable for the entries on the musical performances at a court ceremony on the fifteenth day of the first month (chapter 1, page 349); for a list of members of the court orchestra, grouped according to their instruments (chapter 1, page 354); and for a list of famous entertainers, grouped according to their specialties (chapter 6, pages 453–466).

All the above works are still extant in either Yuan or Ming editions from which several modern editions have been made.[175]

[174] Compare p. 172 with p. 59, and p. 308 with p. 96, of the combined editions of these works (see below, note 175).

[175] In 1956 a group of works on Sonq social life, including the four mentioned in this chapter, were collated with the best available editions, and were published in a single volume, by the Classics Press (古典文學出版社), Shanghai. See also Jaques Gernet, *Daily Life in China on the Eve of the Mongol Invasion* (New York, 1962).

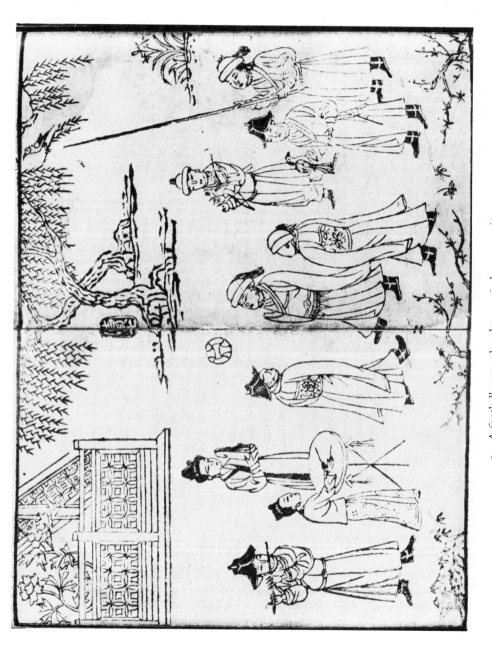

1. A football game played to musical accompaniment

竪簫 橫簫 七星 亳聖 鷓鴣 小孤笛 夏笛 羌笛 官笛

簫管
亳聖鷓鴣
聖鷓鴣久

快屮ㄓ屮屮屮ㄗㄗㄙㄟㄟㄥㄣㄈㄒ久
大尖尖尖尖尖音音音音音音音音音音
ムㄈ字凡凡工人上一五合四一上勾尺工凡六

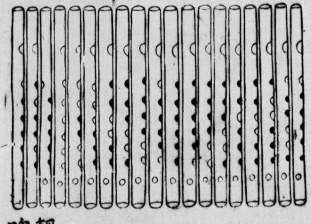

輕吹

2. Diagram of fingerings for the flute

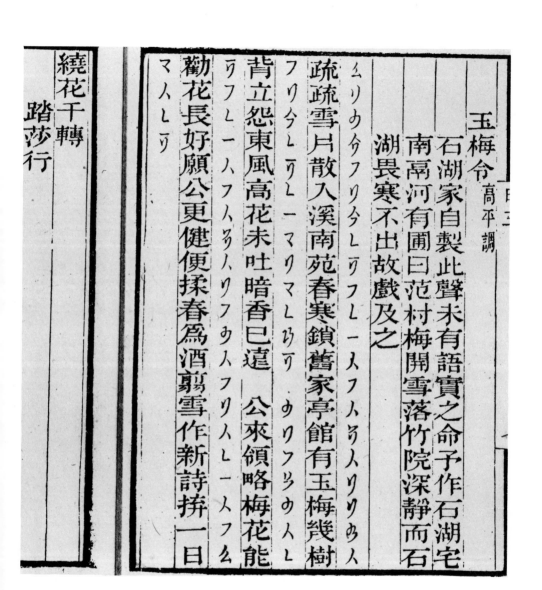

玉梅令　高平調

石湖家自製此聲未有語實之命予作石湖宅
南高河有園曰范村梅開雪落竹院深靜而石
湖畏寒不出故戲及之

ムリめ夕フリ今しリフレ一人フ人ろ人リりめ人
疏疏雪片散入溪南苑春寒鎖舊家亭館有玉梅幾樹
フリ夕しリレ一マリマしめす　ゆリフゐめし
背立怨東風高花未吐暗香已逯　公來領略梅花能
ヲフレ一人フ人ろリフめ人フリめ人しレ一人フム
勸花長好願公更健便揉春爲酒竅雪作新詩拼一日
マ人しリ

繞花千轉

踏莎行

3. The *tsyr* song "Yuhmei Linq" (Jade Plum Blossoms) with music
in the popular notation

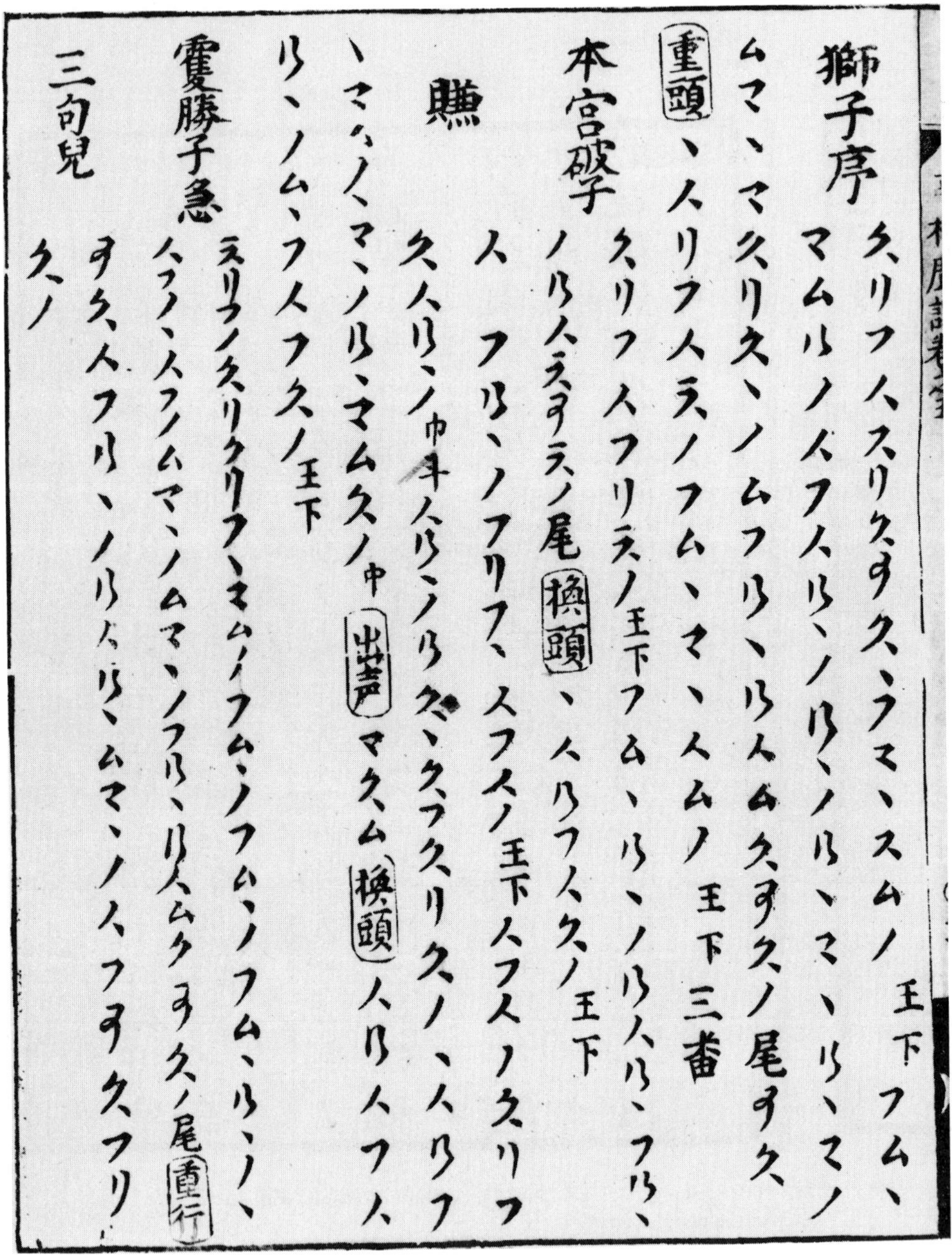

4. *Yuann Cherng Shuang* in the popular notation

願成雙

クリフノ、マム、ｦ 王下 フリフ。人久乃、ノムマ、
、人ゑリ乃。人久乃、ヲリフラゾノ尾 換頭 久リゑ。

願成雙令
、マ。人ゑリ乃、人久乃、
、人リ乃。王下

願成雙慢 フリ乃ノム、ル、ノ久フ尹久ノ 王下、リフ人リ
、ノム、フ人、マ、ノリ久ヲリフノ人リ、ノ
乃、マ、ノ乃、マムノ久尹久ノ尾 換頭 、人リフリ乃ノ
ム、フ人久ノ 王下 巳上係官拍

5. The *chyn* pieces "Jyue Diaw" and "Jyy Diaw" (in part) in tablature form

七月流火九月授衣春日載陽有鳴倉庚女執懿筐遵

彼微行爰求柔桑春日遲遲采蘩祁祁女心傷悲殆及

公子同歸

昏西流卯暑退寒來起夷則七月次黃九月次黃

鍾一之日次大呂二之日次太蔟三之日次夾鍾四

之日自申至卯中虛南呂應

鍾二辰因以爲此章之律調

南
林
仲
林

夾
太
黃
林
仲
林
南

林南無南林仲黃無林無南夾無南林無
南無南林仲黃無林無南夾無南林太無
無夾南林仲林無南無夾無南林太南
南仲林南無太夾無南林無

尺工凡工尺凡
一四合尺上六凡尺合
尺上尺凡工五尺凡

工尺上尺
一四合尺上
尺工凡工尺凡一工五上六凡尺合

6. A stanza of the ceremonial song "In the Seventh Month the Fire Ebbs," with accompaniment of the twenty-five-stringed zither

Chapter II

THE MODAL SYSTEM OF
THE SONQ DYNASTY

I have mentioned in the introduction the importance of modes in the musical theory of the Sonq period; however, the confusion of modal terminology at this time is probably unparalleled in the entire musical history of China. It seems expedient, therefore, before transcribing and examining the actual music, to give as background a theoretical description of the classical and popular modes and an account of their development during the Sonq period.

The Basic Definition of a Mode

In the Sonq period, modes are referred to by two sets of names, popular and classical. Numerous concordances of them can be found in the written sources of the time. *Tsyr Yuan* and *Shyhlin Goangjih,* written at the close of the Sonq, contain the longest lists including a description of the scales of the modes. According to these treatises,[1] a basic scale of seven notes can be constructed, on any one of the twelve pitches within the octave, each made up of the series of Pythagorean fifths generated from that note. For instance, on c, one can produce the scale: c, d, e, f-sharp, g, a, b; or on d: d, e, f-sharp, g-sharp, a, b, c-sharp; and so forth.

In this seven-note scale theoretically each note can be used as the cadencing note of a melody. A mode is thus defined by the pitch on which the basic scale is constructed and by the choice of the cadencing note. Since there are twelve absolute pitches and seven notes in each basic scale, eighty-four modes are theoretically possible. Using c, d-flat, d, and so forth for the Chinese pitch names *hwangjong* 黃鐘, *dahleu*

---

[1] As previously noted, certain sections of these two works may derive from a common source. See Chap. I.

大吕, *taytsow* 太簇,[2] and so forth, and using the Western solmization syllables *fa, sol, la, do, re,* and so forth[3] for the Chinese names of the degrees, *gong* 宮, *shang* 商, *jyue* 角, *jyy* 徵, *yeu* 羽, and so forth, the classical modal names can be expressed in the following manner: *hwang jong-gong* 黃鐘宮, fa of c, meaning that the cadencing note is fa of the (fa) scale which begins on c; *hwang jong-shang* 黃鐘商, sol of c, meaning the cadencing note is sol of the (*fa*) scale which begins on c (that is, d); *dahleu-gong* 大吕宮, fa of d-flat, meaning the cadencing note is fa of the (fa) scale which begins on d-flat (that is, d-flat); *dahleu-shang* 大吕商, sol of d-flat, meaning the cadencing note is sol of the (fa) scale on d-flat (that is, e-flat), and so forth.

However, in presenting the scales of the modes, *Tsyr Yuan* and *Shyhlin Goang jih*[4] make use of the twelve pitch names only in the basic form, which stand for the twelve semitones in the first octave. Although Sonq writings do use such prefixes as *bann* 半 (half), *ching* 清 (high), and *shaw* 少 (small)[5] to modify the pitch names for their octave equivalents, none of these appears in the scales of the so-called Eighty-four Modes in these two treatises. Thus if we read these scales at their face value, all portions that extend beyond b seem to have been transferred back into the first octave. In other words, all modes have nearly the same ambitus (from c, or c-sharp to b, or b-flat), but the intervallic pattern of this scale changes according to the location of the cadencing note. The results in Western notation are shown in Table 2, where the white notes indicate the cadencing notes.[6]

Mention is made in different sections of both treatises of four additional notes in the upper octave, c′, d′-flat, d′, e′-flat. These are called *Syh Gong Ching Sheng* (The Four Octave Notes),[7] and four additional

---

[2] See complete list of pitch names in Chap. III. This use of Western pitch letters is of course arbitrary. The actual pitch in terms of vibration is not taken into consideration.

[3] The syllables are used purely to indicate the intervallic relationship as they are applied to the diatonic scale. They have no absolute pitch significance as in the so-called fixed-do system.

[4] This treatise presents the eighty-four scales twice, once in pitch names and again in the popular notation, which leaves no ambiguity of the octave used.

[5] These are used by Tsay Yuandinq, Jiang Kwei, and Ju Shi respectively. In *SLGJ* (5.62a) there are six compound symbols on the diagram of finger positions on the flute, obtained, apparently, from overblowing. However, they do not appear in the chart of modes nor in the existing musical examples.

[6] Since there are only twelve pitch names given in an octave, sharped and flatted notes are interchangeable enharmonically, for example, f-sharp equals g-flat, and so forth.

[7] I am not certain of the meaning of *gong* here. My translation is based on the explanatory note immediately following this term: "These four octave notes were used only in

symbols in the popular notation are assigned to them.[8] The use of these four notes was sanctioned in a certain type of ceremonial music. According at least to one theorist (as we shall see below),[9] the c′ instead of c is regularly used as a cadencing note. In the Sonq musical examples, both ceremonial and popular, these four higher notes appear quite frequently. However, they do not seem to constitute elements in the basic system of modes here.

In the Northern Sonq period a series of the so-called Twenty-eight Popular Modes appears in Sheen Gua's *Additional Memoirs*.[10] Aside from being a much shorter list, this differs from the set of eighty-four modes in that octave notes are included (though not always forming a full scale); one set of scales (the g group) has a smaller range; and all the mi modes have an extra note (to be explained presently). Yet despite these details, the structure of the two tables is basically similar. (See Table 3.)

A treatise of the seventh century, *Yueh Shu Yaw Luh* 樂書要録,[11] shows a similar concept of modes in the section "On the Theory That All Pitches Establish Their Own Laws of Superiority and Inferiority": "All tubes are low in pitch when they are long and high in pitch when they are short. Supposing the fa [the lowest note of the basic scale] to be on *jyajong* [e-flat], then re will be on *hwangjong* [c]. The fact that the e-flat [tube] is shorter than the c [tube] shows that a fa note is not necessarily always a lower note; and since the c [tube] is longer than the e-flat [tube], a re is not necessarily always a higher note."[12] The important point here is that the cadencing note is not necessarily always the lowest note.

The only Sonq dynasty treatise that gives a radically different interpretation of the modes is *Liuhleu Shin Shu* by Tsay Yuandinq, who seeks to create a scale on every one of the twelve semitones with ident-

---

the Jou dynasty ceremonical music for the Sacrifice to Heaven; the singers and flutists today also borrow these octave notes to form final cadences."

四宮清聲在周禮惟祀天之樂用之，今之樂色管色並用寄四宮清聲煞

[8] See list in Chap. III for the entire set of sixteen symbols.

[9] See Sheen Gua mentioned below. Criticisms by Chern Yang and Ju Shi only show that this must have been a common practice of Sonq times.

[10] Pars. 531, 541. The set of Twenty-eight Popular Modes is mentioned in several other earlier works (see discussion below). However, this has the most detailed description of the scales.

[11] An anonymous work, only three chapters (5, 6, and 7) of which are extant. See Hazuka Keimei, "Commentary on *Gaku-Sho-Yō-Roku*," in *Tōyō Ongaku Kenkyū*, 1940, no. 2.

[12] *Yueh Shu Yaw Luh*, 5.4.

Table 2. The Eighty-four Modes from *Shyhlin Goangjih* and *Tsyr-Yuan*

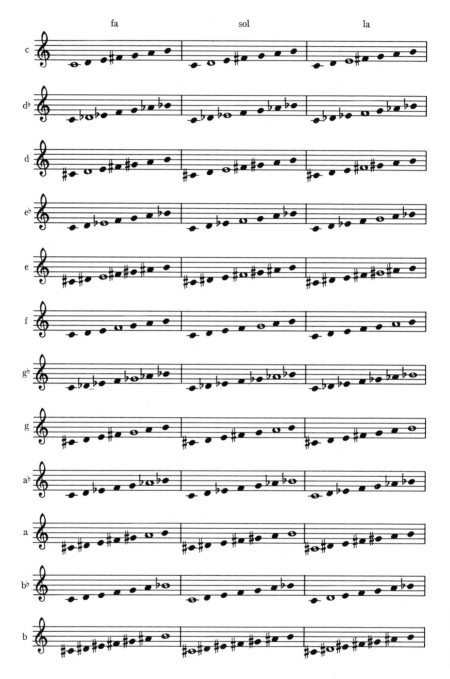

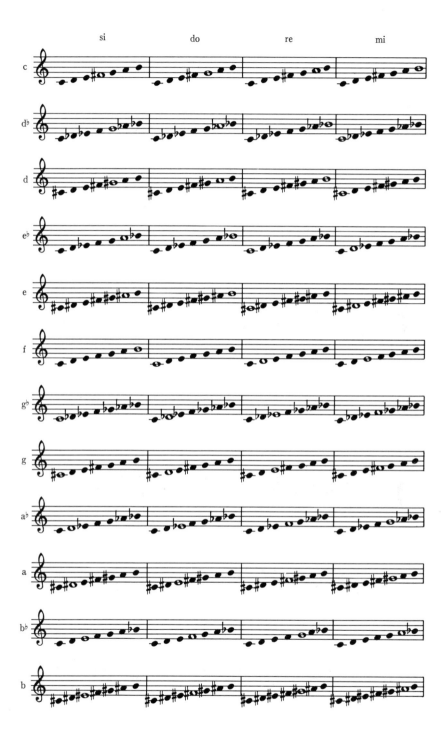

Table 3. Sheen Gua's Twenty-eight Popular Modes

re   mi (la)

c

d♭

e♭

f

g

a♭

b♭

ical intervallic relations.[13] In other words, the note *gong* (fa) should always be at the bottom of the scale. To do this one needs a range of about two octaves. Since Tsay considers only the notes fa, sol, la, do, and re as orthodox cadencing notes, his total number of modes is sixty.[14] It is however doubtful that Tsay's modes were ever widely used.[15] Table 4 shows the series of Tsay's modes in Western notation. The small cross represents notes that are twenty-four cents higher than the original (see Chapter I, note 32). The flatted notes are used interchangeably with the sharped notes here as in Table 2.

Evolution of the Popular Modes

In treatises and music of the Sonq period modes are often referred to only by their popular names. Such names stem from different origins: *pyngdiaw* 平調 and *dawgong* 道宮, for example, are Chinese names of uncertain meaning; *banshehdiaw* 般涉調 and *dahshyrdiaw* 大石調 are adaptations of Sanskrit names;[16] *gau pyngdiaw* 高平調 (higher *pyngdiaw*) and *jonggoan dawgong* 中管道宮 (medium tube *dawgong*) are rationalized Chinese names.[17] Unlike the classical names most of these do not readily indicate the nature of the modes. Some have the appearance of classical names, such as *jongleugong* 中呂宮, *hwangjonggong* 黃鐘宮, and so forth, but can no longer be interpreted in a technical sense, since the meaning of their names has changed. These popular names of modes appear as early as the middle of the Tarng dynasty,[18] and by late Tarng they seem to have been organized into a system of Twenty-eight Modes[19] and are

[13] See Chap. I.

[14] *Liuhleu Shin Shu*, I.7.

[15] Shyong Pernglai in *Seh Puu* tries to follow Tsay's system but not completely (see Chap. I).

[16] *Pañcama, kaiśika.* See Hayashi Kenzō, *Studies on the Modes of Entertainment Music in the Swei and Tarng Periods* (in Chinese), pp. 44, 46.

[17] *Tsyr Yuan* has a popular name for every one of the Eighty-four Modes, many of which are rationalized names added to make the list of popular names correspond to the list of classical names. *SLGJ* has popular names for only forty-eight of the modes. (see above, p. 27.)

[18] In the detailed account of the famous revision of many song titles made by imperial order in the thirteenth year of Tainbao 天寶 (A.D. 754), in *Lii Daw Yaw Jyue* 理道要訣 by Duh Yow 杜佑, the song titles are grouped under fourteen modes, each labeled with both its popular and classical name. (Duh Yow's work is no longer extant, but it was extensively quoted in *Tarng Hueyyaw*. See Kishibe Shigeo, "Twenty-eight Modes," pp. 595–597.

[19] Kishibe believes that the fourteen modes mentioned by Duh Yow are part of the set of twenty-eight. "Twenty-eight Modes," pp. 600–608.

mentioned in such works as *Yueh Shu* 樂書 by Shyu Jiingan 徐景安[20] and *Yuehfuu Tzarluh* by Duann Anjye.[21] In the Northern Sonq dynasty concordances with the classical names can be found in *Jiingyow Yueh Swei Shin Jing* and *Buu Biitarn;* in the Southern Sonq the Twenty-eight Modes were listed by Tsay Yuandinq in his partially preserved *Yannyueh Shu* (Book on Festival Music).[22] By the end of the Sonq period *Tsyr Yuan* and *Shyhlin Goangjih* state: "Today in both ceremonial and popular music only seven fa modes and twelve sol and re modes are preserved; the la modes are excluded."[23]

The term *diaw* 調 has often been used as a general term for all modes. More specifically, however, during Sonq times *diaw* was used for the sol and re modes, *gong* 宮 for the fa modes, and *jyue* 角 for the la modes. These nineteen modes are listed in *Tsyr Yuan* and *Shyhlin Goangjih* only by their popular names. But the concordances in these books gives us the classical names which are listed here along with the other modes (in parentheses) to make up the original set of twenty-eight.[24]

fa of c	sol of c	re of c	(mi of c)
fa of d-flat	(sol of d-flat)	(re of d-flat)	(mi of d-flat)
fa of e-flat	sol of e-flat	re of e-flat	(mi of e-flat)
fa of f	sol of f	re of f	(mi of f)
fa of g	sol of g	re of g	(mi of g)
fa of a-flat	sol of a-flat	re of a-flat	(mi of a-flat)
fa of b-flat	sol of b-flat	re of b-flat	(mi of b-flat)

Although the modes in the last column have since been discarded, the fact that the popular modes with the *jyue* names are grouped as mi modes in *Tsyr Yuan* and *Shyhlin Goangjih* requires further explanation. As noted earlier, the suffix *jyue* was usually associated with the la modes. Indeed, the fragment of the treatise *Jiingyow Yueh Swei Shin Jing* which is quoted in the *Sonq History* (see Chapter I) indicates very clearly, by means of the corresponding classical names, that in the Northern Sonq these "*jyue* modes" were la modes. But the Northern Sonq writer Sheen Gua (*Memoirs,* paragraphs 531, 541) had already described these *jyue* modes as mi modes; he also adds one extra note (see the ones in

[20] The work is also called *Lihday Yueh Yih* 歷代樂議. Large portions of it are preserved in the *New Tarng History,* chap. 22, *Yuh Hae,* chap. 105, and Chern Yang's *Yueh Shu,* chap. 157. (Kishibe, "Twenty-eight Modes," pp. 450–451.)

[21] *Miscellaneous Notes on Music* (a late ninth-century work in one chapter), pp. 41–42.

[22] *Sonq History,* "Monograph on Music," 142.1822a–b.

[23] I have taken the text from *Tsyr Yuan,* I.36. Although the passage is much the same in both sources, the *SLGJ* text is corrupt and some phrases are misplaced.

[24] The characters for the popular names of the modes as given in *Tsyr Yuan* are as

Table 4. Tsay Yuandinq's Sixty Modes using the series of eighteen notes

la   do   re

parentheses in Table 3) to each scale. This practice was noted with dis-approval in the *Sonq History:* "In judging music, one needs only to look at its tone system. The notes mi and si (the seventh and the fourth de-grees on the fa scale) are not the proper tones, yet si has been used for fa, and mi has been used for la, thus confusing the proper tones ... The twenty-eight modes are what Wann Baocharng [萬寶常] (a Tarng court musician) called 'sounds unfit for an era of good government.' Further-more, in the vulgar music one extra note is added to each of the seven *jyue* modes in the most reckless and unrestrained manner, while the original, proper modes are no longer remembered."[25]

Though there is no reason to rule out completely the possibility of scales including a succession of three semitones, the appearance of these extra notes is more likely due to the fact that at some time during the Northern Sonq period the la modes were a fifth higher in practice than they were in theory. In other words, they were on the pitch levels of the mi modes (hence the complaint that "mi has been used for la"), but they retained the la type of interval pattern. The two types of scales differ only in one note: the mi scales having the semitone between the first and second degree, the la scales having it between the second and third. Therefore, the extra note in Table 3, which always occurs one whole tone above the cadencing note, could very well have been the *alternative second-degree note.*[26] Why the transposed la modes (or altered mi modes) were discarded toward the end of the Sonq dynasty is difficult to

follows.

正宮	大石調	般涉調	大石角
高宮	高大石調	高般涉調	高大石角
中呂宮	雙調	中呂調	雙角
道宮	小石調	正平調	小石角
南呂宮	歇指調	高平調	歇指角
仙呂宮	商調	仙呂調	商角
黃鐘宮	越調	羽調	越角
Jenqgong	*Dahshyrdiaw*	*Banshehdiaw*	*Dahshryjyue*
Gaugong	*Gau Dahshyrdiaw*	*Gau Banshehdiaw*	*Gau Dahshyrjyue*
Jongleugong	*Shuangdiaw*	*Jongleudiaw*	*Shuangjyue*
Dawgong	*Sheaushyrdiaw*	*Jenqpyngdiaw*	*Sheaushyrjyue*
Nanleugong	*Shiejyydiaw*	*Gau Pyngdiaw*	*Shiejyyjyue*
Shianleugong	*Shangdiaw*	*Shianleudiaw*	*Shangjyue*
Hwangjonggong	*Yuehdiaw*	*Yeudiaw*	*Yuehjyue*

[25] "On Popular Music", 142.4822b:
觀其律本則其樂可知, 變宮變徵既非正聲而以變徵為宮以變宮為角, 反
紊亂正聲...所收二十八調本萬寶常所謂非治世之音, 俗又於七角調各加
一,聲 流蕩忘反, 而祖調亦不復存矣.
[26] Hayashi Kenzō, *Modes of Entertainment Music,* pp. 76–79, suggests in his study of the

explain. The names, however, have remained associated with the pitch level of the mi modes and are found in *Tsyr Yuan* and *Shyhlin Goang jih*. But in these works the authors no longer bothered to add the extra notes in their description of the modes. Sheen Gua's description of the scales and cadencing notes of the *jyue* modes cannot be questioned, as his spelling of the modes in the *gongcheh* notation is entirely consistent. However, he seems not to have readjusted the original classical names of these modes accordingly; so that if arranged by the meanings of the classical names, Sheen Gua's modes appear exactly as those in *Jiingyow Yueh Swei Shin Jing,* except the cadences of the *jyue* modes are placed a fifth too high, a discrepancy in Sheen's work which has also been noted by Kishibe.[27]

Changes in Meaning of the Classical Names of the Modes

As already noted, the nature of a mode is not indicated by its popular name. The professional musician knew by tradition what mode each name implied. It is for scholars, particularly those of later times, that concordances of the two sets of names are useful. Unfortunately, the pairing of classical and popular names in the various lists is not always the same. If we compare the concordances in *Jiingyow Yueh Swei Shin Jing* and in *Tsyr Yuan,* we find that the Northern and the Southern Sonq works differ in their pairing of certain names. But within each period the lists are in agreement.

Hayashi Kenzō[28] and Kishibe Shigeo[29] have both made extensive studies of this question, and both have proposed the same theory: that there was a change in the method of reading the classical names; for example, *hwang jong-shang* 黃鐘商 is sometimes *hwang jong jy shang* 黃鐘之商 and at other times is *hwang jong wei shang* 黃鐘為商. The Southern Sonq method of reading the classical names which is described in the beginning of this chapter is called by Hayashi and Kishibe the *jy-diaw*

---

la modes the same explanation for the extra notes.

[27] Kishibe, "Twenty-eight Modes," p. 459. An interesting case is found in some of Shyong Pernglai's ceremonial songs, where he has used the popular names of the high la modes but has composed his la melodies in the original key as suggested by the classical names. See further details in the introduction to the transcription of Shyong's songs in Chap. IV, below.

[28] *Modes of Entertainment Music,* pp. 129–138.

[29] Twenty-eight Modes," pp. 587–592.

之調 system, which means that one may insert the word *jy*, a subordinate particle (the English "of" in reverse) in all of the classical modal names; for instance, *hwang jong jy gong* 黃鐘之宮 and *hwang jong jy shang* 黃鐘之商 simply express more specifically "the fa of c," "the sol of c." The authors propose to call the Northern Sonq method the *wei-diaw* 為調 system of nomenclature, because they have found that in the Northern Sonq instead of *jy*, the verb to be, *wei* 為 was implied in the modal names. Thus the full form of the names should be read, for example, *hwang jong wei gong* 黃鐘為宮 or *hwang jong wei shang* 黃鐘為商, meaning literally, "fa being on c," "sol being on c." In the former system the cadences are on c (fa) and d (sol) respectively; in the latter system the cadences are both on c, but play the function of a fa note and a sol note in turn.

As a more specific example, the Southern Sonq treatises state that *dahshyrdiaw* 大石調 corresponds to *hwang jong-shang,* which must be read "the sol of c"; that is, the cadence is on d. Northern Sonq treatises, on the other hand, state that *dahshyrdiaw* is *taytsow-shang* 太簇商. Only if we read this as "sol being d" will the cadence still be on d and the mode remain the same. Naturally, in the case of fa modes "fa being c" and the "fa of c" are the same thing, and therefore, in treatises of both periods, *hwang jong-gong* in the classical nomenclature, for example, corresponds to *jenq gong* 正宮 in the popular nomenclature.

The two characters *wei* and *jy* were not used regularly in treatises. Probably these characters were taken for granted by musicians during both of the Sonq periods, and their omission created new problems for later readers of Sonq works on music.[30]

The Use of Modes in the Sonq Period

The great concern of Sonq musicians with the modes is evident in the frequent discussions of regular and irregular cadences[31] in musical treatises and other literary sources. Well-known Tarng and Sonq mel-

---

[30] We find this kind of misunderstanding of modal names already in Shyong Pernglai's *Seh Puu.* However, his position as a practical musician is questionable in any case (see notes to the transcription in Chap. IV). The comparison of the two systems given by Shiah Jinqguan (*Origins of Tsyr Tunes,* pp. 45–46) is difficult to understand. Fang Cherngpeir (*Chats on the Tsyr,* chap. I, secs. 5–8) tried to correlate without much success the modes of Jiang Kwei's music from the Southern Sonq period with the concordance in the Northern Sonq work *Jiingyow Yueh Swei Shin Jing.* For a list of the popular modal names given in the Northern Sonq arrangement, see Maurice Courant, "Essai historique sur la musique classique des chinois," p. 117.

[31] Cadences are variously called *shasheng* 殺聲 (Sheen Gua, par. 114), *jyesheng* 結聲

odies were usually mentioned together with their modal names, and, as noted earlier, musical anthologies grouped them according to their modal categories.[32]

Numerous reasons are given to explain the importance placed by Sonq musicians on the mode of a piece of music. From an essentially nonmusical point of view, there was of course a long tradition which assigned cosmological significance to the pitches and the degrees of the scales, a tradition still observed in late Sonq times by Yang Shooujai whose *Five Rules for Writing Tsyr* was appended to *Tsyr Yuan* by Jang Yan.[33] Such extramusical associations, however, were less and less observed. The emotional context of the popular modes was expounded by Jou Derching early in the Yuan dynasty (1324),[34] but we do not know how much further back these associations go. On the other hand, the choice of modes in popular music during the Sonq period seemed rather free. The *Sonq History,* for instance, records that Emperor Tay Tzong, the second ruler of the dynasty, rewrote many old melodies in different modes.[35] The writing of *tsyr,* the most outstanding song form of the time, by composing new texts to established melodies certainly often created inconsistencies in the association of music with words.[36]

(*Tsyr Yuan,* I.56), *bihcheu* 畢曲 (Tsay Yuandinq, *Liuhleu Shin Shu,* I.95–105, and so forth). Irregular cadences are of many kinds and are more often enumerated than explained; for instance, Sheen Gua writes (par. 114): "The cadences of the various modes do not always fall on their proper notes; there are *piansha* 偏殺, *tsehsha* 側殺, *jihsha* 寄殺, *yuansha* 元殺, and so forth."

Some of these cadences might be explained from indirect suggestions, but further confirmation is needed. For example, *jihsha* could mean "borrowing the octave note as the cadence" from the context of the passage in *Tsyr Yuan* (I.32). *Tsehsha* might be the term explained in *Bihji Mannjyh* (3.6a): "*linjong-shang* 林鐘商 is *sol* of a-flat. In terms of the flute notation, the cadence should be on the character *farn* [凡; b-flat], but when it is a *tsehshang* [mode; 側商], then the cadence borrows the note *cheh* [尺; g]."

There is also an expression *fann* 犯 mentioned in many treatises, which has been considered an elaborate form of borrowed cadences. It is however a problematic term which may have several meanings. (See the notes to the transcription of No. 16 of Jiang Kwei's songs in popular notation in Chap. IV.)

[32] Such as the list of revised songs of the thirteenth year of Tianbao (see above, note 19), and the Emperor Tay Tzong's new compositions as recorded in *Sonq History* (142.4822c) and in *Yuehfuu Hwencherng* (see above, Chap. I), and so forth.

[33] 2.71. 楊守齋, 作詞五要.

[34] *Jongyuan Inyunn Jenqyeu Tzuohtsyr Chiilih* (Rules for Diction and Composing *Tsyr* in Chinese).

[35] 142.4822c.

[36] Baxter, *Index,* p. 111. For a special discussion of the use of modes in *tsyr,* see Shiah Cherngtaur, "Three Principles of *Tsyr,*" in his *Collection of Essays,* pp. 1–7.

From a practical point of view, a clear indication of the modes would have been convenient for performers—players of the *chyn*[37] and *pyiba,*[38] for example—since the mode of a piece had an important bearing on the tuning of the strings. As we shall see in greater detail in the next chapter, designation of the mode in cases where the notation had ambiguous symbols was useful for players of the flute, an instrument which during the Sonq became more prominent than stringed instruments, and possibly also useful for singers.

Finally, it should be noted that several of the larger Sonq musical forms utilized the modes in their organization. Literary sources show that mode was an important formal element. Each of the *dahcheu* 大曲, a kind of suite involving singing and dancing,[39] and each of the *juann* 賺, a kind of medley,[40] were written in a single prescribed mode. A more elaborate kind of medley, the *jugongdiaw* 諸宮調,[41] a term meaning literally "various modes," is characterized by melodies in groups (*taw-shuh* 套數) of contrasting modes, a formal feature which was later carried over into the Yuan musical drama.[42]

[37] See Jiang Kwei's discussion on tunings for the seven-stringed zither in his *Dahyueh Yih* partially preserved in the *Sonq History,* 4821c–d.

[38] The names of the modes seem to have served also as names of tuning systems in the Japanese collection of biwa (*pyiba*) music of the twelfth century entitled *Sango Yōroku* 三五要録 by Fujiwara no Moronaga 藤原師長 (1138–1192). (There are many manuscript copies, the oldest, dated 1328, being in the Library of the Imperial Household Agency in Tokyo.)

[39] Wang Jwo in *Random Notes* (3.6b) states: "In the *dahcheu* movements *yn, shiuh, mann, jinn,* and *linq* are written in the prescribed mode. This is the normal procedure of those who write *cheu.*" On this subject see also Wang Gwowei, *History of Chinese Drama,* p. 193.

[40] See Wang Gwowei, *History of Chinese Drama,* p. 48, on an example in *SLGJ.*

[41] On the formal details of *jugongdiaw* see Jenq Jenndwo 鄭振鐸, *A Study of the Jugongdiaw of the Sonq, Jin,* and *Yuan Dynasties* (1932), reprinted in his collected works, *Studies in Chinese Literature* 中國文學研究, vol. III, p. 870.

[42] For a literary study of the early forms of musical drama, see Hightower, *Chinese Literature* pp. 85–86.

Chapter III

FORMS OF NOTATION IN SONQ MUSICAL SOURCES

The Popular ·Notation[1]

The popular notation is the notation as described in the theoretical treatises of Jang Yan (*Tsyr Yuan*) and Chern Yuanjinq (*Shyhlin Goangjih*) in the Sonq. It consists of ten basic symbols, five of which may be modified by a circumscribed circle to indicate that the note is to be read a semitone lower, and of these five, one may also be modified by a superscribed hook to indicate that it is to be read a semitone higher than the original. Including these variations, the symbols represent a gamut of sixteen semitones from c to e′-flat:[2]

ㄙ	⊘	ㄋ	⊖	—	ㄥ	<	∧
c	d-flat	d	e-flat	e	f	f-sharp	g
⑦	ㄱ	⑪	刂	久	⑨	ㄥ	ㄥ
a-flat	a	b-flat	b	c′	d′-flat	d′	e′-flat.[3]

[1] Sonq writers refer to this system as *swuyueh jy puu* 俗樂之譜 notation of popular music (Ju Shi), and *jyy tzyhpuu* 指字譜 character notation for the fingers (Jang Yan), Writers of later periods have variously called it *swu tzyhpuu* 俗字譜 the popular character notation (Chern Lii); *yannyueh tzyhpuu* 燕樂字譜 character notation for entertainment music, and *parngpuu* 傍譜 side-notation (Yang Inliou); *Bairshyr puu* 白石譜 Notation of Whitestone [the Taoist] (Shiah Cherngtaur); and many others.

[2] The absolute pitch given here is arbitrary. In his *Additional Memoirs* (par. 532) Sheen Gua says the lowest note equals *hwangjong* (which I have given c), but in his original *Menqshi Memoirs* (par. 114) he says that in actual practice all the pitches are raised approximately three quarters of a tone higher than the orthodox pitches. Since our main concern is with the relative pitch of the notation, the simpler, theoretical equivalents will be adopted. In both theoretical discussions and transcriptions (in Chap. IV), c will stand for middle c, c′ for the note an octave above, C for the octave below, and C_1 for two octaves below. Although I am using the sharped and flatted notes in the Western notation enharmonically, for example, e-flat equals d-sharp, I have used mostly flats in the tables of modes and transcriptions to simulate the relationship between a modified and an unmodified symbol in the popular notation.

[3] In various editions of *SLGJ* and *Tsyr Yuan* the woodcuts of the last four notes are sometimes corrupt. The symbols presented here are the standard forms.

Because they resemble and in Sonq sources are often associated with another set of notational symbols (the *gongcheh* notation, to be discussed later) which can be read as regular Chinese characters, it has become common practice to borrow the pronunciation of the latter—*her, syh, i, shanq, gou, cheh, gong, farn, liow, wuu*[4]—for these less familiar-looking symbols.

In the actual music (Jiang Kwei's Seventeen *Tsyr* Songs, the textless melodies in *Shyhlin Goangjih,* and the three pieces in *Cheu Liuh*), however, the circle does not appear in any of the preserved sources. Furthermore, the hook does not seem to be used in any rational manner. It is impossible to tell whether these aberrations were intentional or accidental.

The inclusion of circle and hook is actually not essential: to decide what the ambiguous symbols stand for, one has only to consult the mode, which was usually specified at the beginning of each piece of music in Sonq times. Among Sonq works Sheen Gua's description of modes (transcribed in Table 3) is the most complete, and from this table one can see that for any given mode only one reading of the ambiguous symbols is possible. Sheen Gua's table differs from the one in *Tsyr Yuan* and *Shyhlin Goangjih* (see Table 2)[5] in that it is the only description of modes that covers the entire gamut of sixteen notes. It includes a choice for *wuu,* the symbol in the highest position, which represents not two but three possible notes. (The probable aid of the hook will be put aside for the moment because of its irregular occurrence.) The choice of one among the three readings in these cases seems to be arbitrary, because the lower portion of the scales shows that two readings of the three are often theoretically possible. It is also to be noted that the result of this selection of only one note often produces a gap of a minor third at the higher portion of the scale. The question is, how is the specific note at the higher position decided upon? And if its selection is strictly determined, why is the hook ever necessary?

I would like to consider these problems in the light of a closer examination of some actual music, specifically, Jiang Kwei's set of Seventeen *Tsyr* Songs which are written in the popular notation (transcribed

---

[4] The syllables given here correspond to the popular symbols only in their basic form. On method of referring to the modified notes see discussion on the *gongcheh* notation below.

[5] Tsay Yuandinq's modes in Table 4, being purely hypothetical and never associated with the popular notation, need not concern us in this case although they too use a scale of only one octave.

in Chapter IV). As indicated by the labels, these songs are in three basic types of modes: the fa modes (Numbers 6, 7, 10, 11, 12), the re modes (Numbers 1, 4, 8, 16), and the sol modes (Numbers 2, 3, 5, 9, 15, 17). There is one piece in the do mode (Number 14), and one in the la mode (Number 13), but these are Jiang Kwei's experiments in theoretical modes which were not in current use.

Looking at the fa-mode melodies in terms of the diagrams of melodic analysis and the schemes of cadences (Tables 5 and 6) we find that they do not all use the same scale, but they share the common characteristic of having secondary cadences (where rhyming occurs in the text) mostly on the major third above and the minor third below the final cadences (indicated by a double fermata), and occasionally on their octave equivalents. The melodic movements (as shown by the slurs) reinforce this pattern by the predominant use of the major and minor third formed by the final and the secondary cadencing notes within the phrases. When the prescribed ambitus of the mode allows, another minor third is usually added, forming a series of thirds, minor-major-minor, beyond which there is often a repetition of one of the minor thirds at the upper or lower octave. The other notes which do not form these thirds in the melody are more ornamental in function, and similar to the use of the passing tone (for example, the f and a in Numbers 6 and 7, the c in Number 12), the auxiliary note (the b-flat in Numbers 10 and 11), the appoggiatura (b-flat in Numbers 10, 11), the cambiata (a in Number 6, f in Number 7), and so forth. If these characteristics are typical of fa modes, it seems that the ambiguous note *wuu* in melody 6 should then be read e'-flat. Melody Number 7 does not have a *wuu* hence the question does not arise. In melodies 10 and 11, which also have the ambiguous symbol *wuu*, the series of thirds is located higher on the scale. Theoretically, the note d is possible in Numbers 10 and 11, functioning in a manner similar to the note a in Numbers 6 and 7. However, the symbol *wuu* in Numbers 10 and 11 appears at octave jumps or at the beginning of a new phrase, positions not comparable to the ornamental use of a in Numbers 6 and 7, and so e'-flat seems the more likely note. Number 12 is in a mode without an e'-flat; there all symbols for *wuu* are automatically read d'.

The melodies in the re modes, comprising Numbers 1, 4, 8, and 16, are also built on a series of thirds, minor-major-minor. They differ from the previous group in that the final note in each is on the lowest note of the series of thirds while the secondary cadences are frequently on the

Table 5. Diagrams of melodic analysis of the Seventeen *Tsyr* Songs by Jiang Kwei

Table 6. Schemes of secondary and final cadencing notes on rhymed words in the
Seventeen *Tsyr* Songs by Jiang Kwei

The re modes

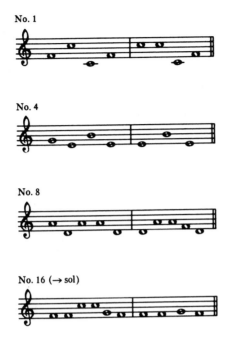

No. 1

No. 4

No. 8

No. 16 (→ sol)

minor third and the fifth above the final. Note that Numbers 1 and 16 share the same scale with Numbers 10 and 11 (see Table 1), and in fact, Number 16 even resembles Numbers 10 and 11 in large portions of the melody. In this group only Numbers 1 and 16 contain the ambiguous symbol *wuu*. In Number 16 *wuu* appears mostly at the beginning of a phrase. Since an initial note is more likely to be a functionally important note, e′-flat is the better choice. In Number 1 the *wuu* is in the position of an auxiliary note which can be either a stepwise figure or a skipping figure of a minor third. Here, too, because of the predominatly tertial quality of the melody, e′-flat seems more suitable.

The third group, in the sol modes, differs from the two previous groups in that the secondary cadences are mostly situated at a fourth below and a second above the final. Although the intervals of the thirds also occur frequently, they do not appear to be so well organized as the series of thirds in the melodies of the re and fa modes. On the other hand, the diagrams of melodic movements show a predominance of the major second and a few occurrences of the major fourth. The situation is more explicable if we take into consideration the destination of the melodic motives, which is often really a major fourth with one or two passing notes in between. By this interpretation, we find that the most prominent fourth is just the one formed by the final and the lower secondary cadence. In some melodies two or more additional fourths are discernible by this method, and the overlapping of these fourths resulted in the stepwise movements shown in the analytical diagrams.

In this sol group Numbers 17 and 5 make use of the symbol *wuu*. In the former case the pattern of melodic intervals suggests that d′ is more suitable than e′-flat. This piece offers another strong reason for reading *wuu* as d′. As indicated in Table 1 Number 17 has some material in common with Number 9, which is also a sol mode but in a different scale without ambiguous notes. The corresponding passages (in Number 9, the third rhyming line in the first stanza, and the first rhyming line in the second stanza; in Number 17, the second rhyming line in both stanzas) show that d′ is certainly the correct choice. Number 5 is a more irregular piece. But the emphasis on stepwise movement and the predominant use of d in the lower octave support the choice of d′ for *wuu* at the upper octave.

To conclude: the choice thus made for the symbol *wuu* in the five melodies in the fa and re groups agrees with Sheen Gua's scales (Table 3). The gap in these scales must have been due to the nature of the melodies usually associated with the modes, namely the series of thirds. But this does not apply in the case of the sol-mode melodies, which move in fourths and seconds. The choices made according to the melodic analysis for Numbers 5 and 17 do not agree with Sheen Gua's scale for these modes. My suggestion is that Sheen Gua's table of modes is still a partially theoretical one. The scales are based on some tertial and some quartal melodies, and the rest, for example, scales for sol of e-flat and sol of a-flat, are filled in by analogy. It was the resulting inconsistency between Sheen's table and actual music that made it necessary to introduce the hook in the notation.

I have checked through the *Chyangtsuen Tsorngshu* edition of Jiang Kwei's songs for the symbol *wuu* to see how often and where the hooked symbol appears. The choices made through analysis agree with this particular edition seventeen times out of twenty-eight. However, in view of the extensive re-editing of all extant editions—including this one—such a comparison is not very significant.

There is one more detail which deserves attention. In the modes on the g scale the lowest note, which theoretically should be c-sharp, is omitted in every case. The same note at the octave is also omitted. A possible musical explanation for this omission is that some of these g-scale modes may have been of long standing, and because of their established pitch position it was found they best fitted into the row of g scales in the mode system represented by Sheen Gua's table.[6] However, the actual music in these g-scale modes could have been pentatonic, a characteristic which is true of the two short songs in the sol of g mode quoted in *Cheu Liuh,* where there is a five-note introduction, "Shiau-sheng Puu" 娟聲譜, which is merely a short phrase to establish the mode like the *netori* in *gagaku* (see Chapter I and the preliminary remarks to the transcription of this piece in Chapter IV). If such were the case, c-sharp and g would be unnecessary in the scales. Nevertheless the g may have been retained for the sake of uniformity in the modal system. The c-sharp is more troublesome. This note, which can also be read d-flat, would have to use the same symbol that represents d-natural. Its inclusion in the scale would then be confusing as well as useless.

The Secondary Symbols in the Popular Notation

Besides these basic symbols of the popular notation, we find in Sonq sources mention of other symbols which, according to various authors, stand for melodic and rhythmic modification; for example, *Shyhlin Goangjih* has a chart that shows the use of a sign which can be combined with a basic symbol to indicate its octave note.[7] However, it does not occur in the actual music in *Shyhlin Goangjih*. *Tsyr Yuan* lists some symbols with names that suggest their meanings but gives no musical examples to illustrate their use:[8]

勽	for *sheau-juh* 小住	small pause
川	for *cheh* 掣	reduction
勽	for *jer* 折	deflection
㇒	for *dah-juh* 大住	big pause
ㄅ	for *daa* 打	strike.

Jiang Kwei's *tsyr* songs use many compounds formed by joining a basic symbol with various kinds of secondary symbols such as:

[6] One of the g-scale modes (sol of g) *shiejyydiaw,* originally called *shoeidiaw* 水調, may be traced back to the Fourteen Modes of the Tianbao period of Tarng (eighth century). See Kishibe, "Twenty-eight Modes," p. 601.

[7] For example, 㘦, 㐅 are an octave higher than —, 㐅 (*SLGJ,* p. 62a). These modified symbols appear with the fingering chart for the flute, in which overblowing is specified and the *gongcheh* words say: *jian-i* 尖一, *jian-shanq* 尖上 (high e, high f).

[8] I.65.

ㄅ, ㄚ, ㄱ, ㄆ, ノ,

but he gives no explanations. The last two of these also appear in the short pieces in *Cheu Liuh,* and the very last one also in *Shyhlin Goangjih,* in the form of an independent symbol. Sonq treatises discussed these secondary symbols in terms of their descriptive names, and in recent years many writers have tried to correlate these verbal descriptions with some of the symbols in Jiang Kwei's music.[9] However, given the uncertainty of the forms of the symbols both in the music and in the treatises, which have gone through many printings, such correlations can remain only conjectural. In 1957 Yang Inliou approached the problem systematically by studying the positions occupied by each symbol in the music. In the final, realized form his interpretation of the symbols is partly based upon the embellishing methods used in the performance of *kuencheu,* the type of musical drama that is said to preserve many old traditions in singing. Yang formulated a set of rules for the melodic and rhythmic embellishments which he then applied to the secondary symbols in Jiang Kwei's *tsyr* songs.[10]

In the following pages I shall group together some Sonq dynasty and later annotations on the terms indicating melodic modifications. The descriptions are for the most part too general to be applied to the transcriptions in Chapter IV, with the exception of the sign in *Shyhlin Goangjih,* the function of which is quite obvious in the music itself.

The *juh* 住 (pause) is mentioned together with *duen* 敦 (probably also a pause) by Sheen Gua, who says that it is equal to one note, and that a "big pause" is equal to two notes.[11] Jang Yan, also mentioning the two terms together, says that the big and the little pauses are made at the rhyming words.[12] Yang Inliou's statistics show that three of Jiang Kwei's secondary symbols most often appear in the music at places where pauses—large or small—(note that they are quite different from the *sheau-juh* and *dah-juh* of *Tsyr Yuan*) are fitting.[13] And since the first of

[9] Notably, works by Day Charnggeng, Tarng Lan, Shiah Cherngtaur, Chiou Chyong-suen.

[10] See *Studies,* pp. 15-17. A sample of Yang's transcription will be given in Chap. IV. Chiou Chyongsuen's study, which emphasizes the rhythmic interpretation of these symbols, uses ornaments mostly at the same places as in the Yang transcription. However, they are often on different pitches.

[11] *Additional Memoirs,* par. 538:
一敦一住各當一字, 大字住當二字.

[12] *Ibid.*

[13] Of the 251 compounds formed with these three symbols, 133 occur at the end of

these three symbols is used at the rhymed endings far more frequently than the other two (79 out of 133), Yang considers this to be the symbol for the big pause and the other two to be variant forms of the little pause.[14]

The *cheh* 掣 (reduction) according to Sheen Gua[15] "results in one less note"; Jang Yan says that when there is a "reduction" the tempo of the passage must be quick.[16] In other words, it is a reduction in time value. However, *cheh* is used in *Shyhlin Goangjih* in a very different context, which although vague, seems to deal with pitch rather than time.[17]

The *daa* 打 (strike) according to *Shyhlin Goangjih* means that two notes in succession are indicated.[18] Consequently, Yang thinks it corresponds to the present-day practice of repeating a note on the flute by tapping the lowest covered hole.[19]

The *jer* 折 (deflection) is more fully discussed in Sonq works than the other ornaments. The earliest mention of it is again by Sheen Gua: "and there is also the deflection, which is not used for the note *her* [the lowest, that is, c]. It can be a deflection of one fraction [ten percent?], two fractions, or even as many as seven to eight fractions. There are degrees in the distance the fingers are lifted[20] and in the strength of the breath. For instance, the mouth organ and the flute depend entirely upon breathing, while the strings depend only upon pressure of the hand."[21]

In the sections on the "Correct and Incorrect Ways to Make a Cadencing Note," *Shyhlin Goangjih* and *Tsyr Yuan* describe deflection more specifically.[22] "Fa of a-flat concludes on a-flat; it should be [per-

---

rhyming lines (a *yunn* 韻), 29 occur at the end of nonrhyming lines (a *jiuh* 句), 49 at the caesura within the line (a *dow* 逗), and 40 at other places (*Studies*, p. 29).

[14] However, Yang has not been consistent in assigning time values to the pauses. Usually he doubles or triples the length of the notes at these pauses.

[15] *Additional Memoirs*, par. 538: 一掣減一字.

[16] *Tsyr Yuan*, I. 67: 反掣用時須急過. There is no other explanation for the term *faan* 反.

[17] 5.69a: 掣聲下隔一宮; p. 69b: 折掣四相生.

[18] 5.69a: 丁 [打] 聲上下相同.

[19] *Studies*, p. 31.

[20] This technique is still used on the flute in Japanese court music today. When the finger hovers closely over the hole without actually covering it, the player can produce a note as much as a whole tone higher than the note that would be sounded if the hole were covered.

[21] *Additional Memoirs*, p. 538: 更有折聲, 唯合字無, 折一分, 折二分, 至於折七八分者皆是, 舉指有深淺用氣有輕重, 如笙簫則全在用氣, 絃聲只有抑按.

[22] *SLGJ*, 5.61a–b; *Tsyr Yuan*, I. 56–58.

formed] straight and fairly high; if it should be executed with a slight deflection, then it becomes b-flat, which intrudes upon the cadencing note of fa of b-flat . . . Fa of g concludes on g, and it should be level; if the note is deflected then it becomes e, which will intrude upon the cadencing note of re of g."[23] The passage shows that the deflection is an upward or downward melodic movement of varying degrees, but no more exact description of the technique of *jer* exists.[24]

Yang Yinnliou finds that Jang Yan's symbol for deflection appears in the songs of Jiang Kwei most often during an ascending or descending stepwise movement. In *kuencheu* music such places often have a sign calling for an extra quick note in the opposite direction from the melodic progression, somewhat similar to the échappée in the use of nonharmonic tones in Western music. The purpose of this practice, according to the theory of *kuencheu,* is to bring out the linguistic tones of the individual words in the text.[25] Yang has found, however, that in the *tsyr* songs Jiang Kwei does not apply this principle consistently to his text. Therefore it is assumed that these melodic embellishments are of purely musical interest. When the symbol for deflection occurs on repeated notes, Yang regards it simply as an auxiliary note; and because in general all the deflections are shorter (and rhythmically weaker) notes, he sometimes reads the deflection sign as an indication to modify the time value of a note.

The term *jertzyh* 折字 (to deflect a note), which is used and explained by Jiang Kwei himself in his Nine Songs for Yueh, seems to present a special case. He explains:[26] "The flutes use deflected notes. If the preceding note is the deflected note and the following one is b-flat, then it is

---

[23] *Tsyr Yuan:* 仙呂宮是ㄱ字結聲用平直而微高, 若微折而下, 則成川字即犯黃鐘宮...南呂宮是ㅅ字結聲用平而去, 若折而下, 則犯一字, 即犯高平調.

[24] See also commentary by Tsay Jen in *Tsyr Yuan,* pp. 51–68.

[25] This ornamental note used in a descending melody is called a *huo* 豁. When the given notes are, say d–c and a small sign ⌣ is placed under the d, then the performer is to sing d–e–c, allotting to e a fraction of the time originally given to d. (In the case of a–g, the notes actually performed would be a–c'–g, the interpolated notes being usually those of the pentatonic scale.) In an ascending melody, the ornamental note is called a *huoh* 霍, *luoh* 落, or *duen* 敦. For further details, see Wang Jihlieh *Conversations at the Earth Worm Hut* (1928) I.1.38a–b; also Y. R. Chao, "Tone, Intonation, Singsong, Chanting, Recitative, Tonal Composition and Atonal Composition in Chinese." Yang also uses the cambiata (the ornamental note in the direction of the melodic movement but jumping beyond the next note of the melody), which is also common in *Kuencheu.* See, for example, Yang's transcription of "Tzueyynshang Sheaupiin," Number 3 of Jiang Kwei's *tsyr* songs.

[26] II.5a: 簫笛有折字, 假如上折字下無字即其聲比無字微高, 餘皆以下字為準, 金石弦匏無折字, 取同聲代之. See also Picken, "Nine Songs," pp. 217–218.

slightly higher than b-flat, while the other instruments will follow the lower note [that is, b-flat]. The metal, stone, string, and gourd instruments do not use the deflected note; instead they substitute for it the undeflected pitch." Picken has emphasized this microtonal difference between the flutes and other instruments, likening it to the clashes found in present-day *gagaku*.[27] Yang considers it to have been the type of unaccentuated dissonant combinations freqeuntly found in heterophonic performances.[28]

The figure ╱ , which occurs in combination with other symbols in the Seventeen *Tsyr* Songs, is not illustrated in the Sonq treatises. Because it has the same shape as an ancient character it has been identified by Tarng Lan with *juay* (or *yih*) 拽 (drag or pull).[29] This term is mentioned, together with the deflection, in *Tsyr Yuan;*[30] Yang therefore believes that it must also be an ornamental symbol in a rhythmically unstressed position. According to Yang's survey of the *tsyr* songs, the sign combines most frequently with the preceding note in various skips upward or, more commonly, downward. Yang believes that at skips this sign represents one or more passing notes, depending on the size of the skip.[31]

The use of this same symbol is different in *Shyhlin Goangjih,* where it does not appear in combination with other symbols. The music here has no text to help determine its phrasing. But if the symbol is treated as a kind of hold or rest, the result reveals interesting features that help justify this interpretation. First, in every one of the seven pieces the note just before this extra symbol is *liow* (c′), a note which coincides with the final of the prescribed mode given in the beginning (*hwang jong-gong* 黃鐘宮, that is, fa of c).[32] Second, the phrasing of the melodies which result from these holds or rests is musically justified and even seems quite appropriate to some of the given titles, either in style or form. For instance, in the melody called "Shuangshenq Tzyy Jyi" 雙勝子急 (*jyi* meaning literally "agitated" or "hurried," although in its use here it may have already acquired a more technical meaning) it punctuates

---

[27] Picken, "Nine Songs," pp. 217–218.

[28] Yang, *Studies,* p. 23.

[29] Tarng, *A Study o the Side Notation,* p. 66.

[30] I.67: 折拽悠悠带漢聲 (The "deflection" and the "drag" or "pull" are delicate, with suggestions of the sound of Hann).

[31] In his transcription Yang supplies as many as three or four passing tones within such skips. See his *Studies,* p. 54, line 1, bar 4, the original notes b to d on the character *an tzay* 安在; and p. 59, line 1, bar 5, g to f-natural on the characters *shoei moh* 水陌.

[32] There are also other interesting problems concerning the mode of these melodies which will be discussed later.

many phrases that are short and repetitive. In the last piece, "San Jiuh erl" 三句兒 (Three Lines), this symbol marks precisely the endings of the three phrases.

On the subject of rhythm, little can be learned from the treatises. Several noteworthy passages are given in *Tsyr Yuan* and *Shyhlin Goangjih,* and occasional comments are also found in Wang Jwo's *Random Notes* and so forth, but they are not explained in sufficiently concrete terms to be of help in the present transcriptions.

Turning to the musical examples, Jiang Kwei's *tsyr* songs, as noted earlier, have pauses mostly after the rhyme or other phrase and line endings of the poem. This indicates that the melodic phrasing is closely related to the form of the text. Whether this relationship fits into a general framework of meter, with notes of simple proportions as adopted by Yang Inliou in his transcriptions,[33] or presupposes a rubato-like, free rhythm, such as one hears in the present-day traditional style of chanting poetry,[34] is difficult to determine. On the other hand, the typical features of the *tsyr*—that is, nonsymmetrical stanzas of long and short lines made up of a mixture of odd and even numbers of equally stressed syllables, and the numerous prescribed patterns, each idenfified by a name—[35] are really suggestive of the additive rhythm of the Near East, which is also characterized by prescribed rhythmic formulas of nonsymmetrical patterns.[36] This idea is, of course, merely speculative and needs further study. Nevertheless, it should be pointed out that the concept that Far Eastern music has only "square rhythm"[37] finds support neither in ancient nor in present-day Chinese music.

Unlike the *tsyr* of Jiang Kwei, which are highly sophisticated art songs, the medley in *Shyhlin Goangjih* which as a unit is also called a *juann* 賺 is a genre of a more popular nature. We know that its melodies each had a distinct rhythmic character and that the singer accompanied himself on a percussive instrument,[38] as described in the section "Advice

---

[33] Yang has transcribed all seventeen songs in 4/4 time. Transcription of these songs into the regular duple meter has also been done by Chiou and Picken, although the distribution of time in the various versions are quite different. Picken's work, which came to my attention only during the proof stage of the present study, is a special essay on the rhythmic interpretation of these songs.

[34] A sample of poetic chanting in the present-day traditional style is given in the language recording *The Mandarin Primer,* by Y. R. Chao, FP8002, Folkways Records, New York, 1956, Lesson 22.

[35] Hightower, *Chinese Literature,* p. 80.

[36] Curt Sachs, *Rhythm and Tempo,* p. 25 and chap. 5.

[37] *Ibid.,* chap. 3, "The Far East."

[38] The Yuan edition of *SLGJ* has a woodcut illustration of what seems to be a football game played to the accompaniment of a drummer, a clapper, and a flutist. The preceding

on Singing by the Ehyun Society" from *Shyhlin Goangjih*: "Before he begins, the singer should hold the clappers before his chest but not higher than the nose. He should follow the drum and strike [?] three beats to commence the introduction and then sing the first line."[39]

This set of seven melodies given in the popular notation in *Shyhlin Goangjih* are without text. We can only depend on the sign ⌐, for hold or rest mentioned above for melodic phrasing. In the first melody there are several small circles within a sentence, probably to indicate further subdivisions; only at two places do these coincide with the sign⌐ of the bigger melodic phrasing. At the end of the second melody there is a note saying, "The music above uses the *guan-pai* 官拍."[40] On this term, the name of a kind of beat, the *Tsyr Yuan* comments briefly: "The *guan-pai* and the *yann-pai* 豔拍 differ in strength."[41]

An account of how to sing the *juann* is also given in this chapter of *Shyhlin Goangjih*. The obscurity of the terms makes the whole passage quite difficult to understand, but the last sentences seem clear enough:[42] "In the concluding section of the music there are altogether twelve beats. The first phrase has four, the second has five, and the third has three, thus ending the melody. This is an absolute and unalterable rule." As noted above, the concluding section of the medley in *Shyhlin Goang-jih*, which we assume to be a *juann*, called "San Jiuh'erl," is in three phrases, with six, seven, and seven notes to each phrase. How these notes are to be distributed within each phrase is not explained in the work and may have been left to the judgment of the performer.

In several Sonq works rhythm is mentioned in connection with the *dahcheu*.[43] One can be almost certain that an intimate *tsyr* song would have a rhythmic character different from that of the *dahcheu* or other similar kinds of dance suite with vocal accompaniment. There is no example of this type of music extant today;[44] but from accounts in Sonq works, the use of different kinds of rhythm seem to have been the most outstanding musical feature of this genre. The following passage from

---

text shows clearly that a *juann* is being sung for the occasion.

[39] 5.16, "Ehyun Yawjyue" 遏雲要訣:
假如未唱之初執拍當胸, 不可高過鼻, 須假鼓板, 村掇三拍起引子, 唱頭一句…

[40] 已上係官拍.

[41] I.63: 官拍艷拍分輕重.

[42] 5.16: 尾聲總十二拍, 第一句四拍, 第二句五拍, 第三句三拍煞, 此一定不踰之法.

[43] Besides *SLGJ* see also Wang Jwo's *Random Notes*, 3.7b and 4.1a.

[44] On the form and history of the *dahcheu*, see Yang Yinnliou, *History*, pp, 134, 216–218. On the *dahcheu* as a literary form and especially for some of the specialized terms, see Wang Gwowei, *History of the Dance-suite*, pp. 189–191.

Tsyr Yuan will illustrate the point:[45]

The beat of the *faacheu* 法曲 is like the beat of the *dahcheu* in that each section is different; the fastness and the slowness of the musical notes are adjusted according to the beat. For example, the suite "Shyang Hwanglong Huashyrluh 降黃龍花十六 should have sixteen beats [in each section?]. In the beginning section and middle section there are six notes to a beat. If necessary, the music must stop to wait for the beat; and to steal a breath, one must be nimble. In the concluding section one should use three notes to a beat because the music is coming to an end. In the last few concluding phrases one should cause the notes to waver in order to give the impression that one is reluctant to stop, wishing instead to let the music still linger around the roof beams. The only difference is that in the *faacheu* the introduction has no beats; only in the middle section, where there is singing, do the beats begin. In the *faacheu*, the *dahcheu*, and the *manncheu* 慢曲 the singers beat with their hands, while in the *charnlinq* 纒令 clappers are used.

A few words must also be said about the expressions used for indicating the form of the melodies in *Shyhlin Goangjih*. The characters *huanntour* 換頭, *chorngtour* 重頭, *wang (?) shiah* 王下, *woei* 尾, *san-fan* 三番, and so forth, are written in the music and presumably are used to indicate various methods of repetition. The chart below shows their location in the pieces.

1 _____	_____		_____	_____
	wang shiah		*woei, huanntour*	*wang shiah*
2 _____	_____			
	wang shiah		*woei, huanntour*	*wang shiah*
3 _____	_____			
	wang shiah		*woei, chorngtour*	*wang shiah, san-fan*
4 _____	_____			
	wang shiah		*woei, huanntour*	*wang shiah*
5 _____	*(jindoou) (jong)*			
	wang shiah	*(chusheng)*	*huanntour*	*wang shiah*
6 _____				
			woei, chorngshyng	
7 _____				

---

[45] II.14-15: 法曲之拍與大曲相類, 每片不同, 其聲字疾徐拍以應之, 如大曲降黃龍花十六, 當用十六拍, 前袞中袞六字一拍, 要停聲待拍, 取氣輕巧, 煞袞則三字一拍, 蓋其曲將終也, 至曲尾數句, 使聲字悠揚, 有不忍絕響之意, 似餘音繞梁為

The characters *jindoou* (?) 巾斗, *jong* 中, and *chusheng* 出聲 which are used in Number 5 also appear in a previous section of the same chapter in *Shyhlin Goangjih*.[46] Unfortunagely, though the passage seems to be relevant to the melodies under discussion, the phrases are so cryptic that the text is very difficult to understand without a knowledge of the technical terms used.

The other terms seem to be easier to explain. *Huanntour* (literally, changed head or variant beginning) has been defined by the Ming scholar Wang Jihder as follows: "In the *cheu* songs the second section is labeled *iau* ㄠ by the Northern School and *chyanchiang* 前腔 or *huanntour* 換頭 by the Southern School. *Chyanchiang* means that the two stanzas in succession do not differ from each other by even a single note. On the other hand, *huanntour* means that the beginning section of the melody is altered during the repetition and that there is a slight addition or reduction of the notes."[47] This description seems to fit the present case very well because in each melody the section of music after the words *huanntour* is approximately the same length as the beginning section before the words *wang shiah*, although the two sections differ in the notes and phrasing. With the exception of Number 1, all the variant beginnings cadence on the same note as the corresponding phrase in the first stanza.[48]

No explanation or even mention of the term *wang shiah* has been found in theoretical or practical sources.[49] The two positions where it

佳, 惟法曲散序無拍, 至歌頭始拍, 若唱法曲, 大曲, 慢曲當以手拍, 纏令則用板拍.

[46] 5.16b, "The Art of Singing by the Ehyun Society."

[47] *Cheu Liuh*, 1.7b:　曲之第二調北曰ㄠ南曰前腔曰換頭, 前腔者連用二首一字不易者是也, 換頭者換其前曲之頭而稍增減其字. So far, this is the earliest definition found. A fuller account can be found in the slightly later Japanese work *Gakkaroku* [A Musician's Notes] by Abe Suenao, 13.41.488; and also in the more recent work *Guu Jin Tsyr Huah* 古今詞話 (1689) by Sheen Shyong 沈雄, "Huanntour" 換頭. Sheen claims to have quoted directly from the Sonq work *Tsyr Yuan*, which actually uses the term *guohpiann* 過片 rather than *huanntour*. Tsay Jen, in his recent annotation of *Tsyr Yuan* (II.19), states that the two terms really refer to the same thing. The term *chorngtour* appears many times in the tenth-century *Duenhwang Codex of Pyiba Music*. But its use seems to be somewhat different from the present case. See Hayashi Kenzō, "A Study of the Ancient Notation for the *P'i-pa*," pp. 33–37.

[48] This characteristic of having variant beginnings in the subsequent stanza is already seen in the Seventeen Tsyr Songs of Jiang Kwei, but there, since both the music and the text of the second stanzas are fully written out, the brief instructions for repetition are obviously not necessary.

[49] The single character *wang* 王 also appears in the *Duenhwang Codex*. Cf. Hayashi Kenzō, "Ancient Notation for the *p'i-pa*," pp. 34–35.

appears in each melody suggest that it might be an abbreviated form of the expression *woang shiah* 往下, which in present-day language still means "henceforth."[50] In other words, the term probably tells the performer, "From this point on, continue with the same old melody."

In melody Number 3 the term *chorngtour* 重頭 (literally, repeat head) appears. This should mean an identical repetition, but a variant beginning is still given. However, at the very end of this piece is an additional expression, *san-fan* 三番 (three times). This may mean the melody is to be performed three times, the second time with identical repetition and the third time with the variant beginning. In Number 6 no variant beginning is given. The characters *chorngshyng* 重行[51] are either a corrupted form of *chorngtour* or another way of indicating an exact repetition.

The character *woei* 尾 (literally, tail, end) which appears in Numbers 1, 2, 3, 4, and 6, is in many works discussed not as a portion of a melody but as a name for an entire piece.[52] Wang Jihder, for instance, defines the term: "The concluding melody is called *woei sheng* 尾聲 (tail sound)."[53] In fact, the last piece in the set of melodies in *Shyhlin Goangjih,* "San Jiuh'erl," is the very example cited in the fourteenth-century work *Shyrsan Diaw Nancheu Injye Puu* 十三調南曲音節譜[54] as a standard concluding melody, specifically for musical suites in the *hwangjong-gong* (fa of c) mode. This citation does not, however, help to explain the occurrence of the single character *woei* at the end of each melody in the present case. The word may have been used here simply to indicate more clearly the end of each piece after the repetitions.

The Chyn Tablature

Among the musical sources included in the present survey are seven pieces written in the form of tablature for the *chyn*.[55] These are the

---

[50] In pronunciation, 王 *wang* and 往 *woang* today differ only in the linguistic tones.

[51] The edition of 1418 has 種行.

[52] The earliest mention is probably in the Yuan work *Jy An's Discourse on Singing* (p. 2)

[53] *Cheu Liuh*, I.8a: 煞曲曰尾聲.

[54] This is a work containing a collection of titles of *cheu* songs which has been incorporated into the work *Music of the Cheu Songs* by Wang Jihder. For a study on the date of this work, see Aoki Masaru "History of Chinese Drama of the Recent Centuries," II. 546. The term given in the *Wang Jihder* edition is really *San Jiuh'erl Sha* 三句兒煞 (*sha* meaning "to conclude").

[55] Shyong Pernglai explains a few *chyn* tablature symbols in his *Seh Puu* with illustrations. Presumably they are the fingerings also used on the *seh,* the 25–stringed zither. However, the music itself is written in a tonal notation with *liuhleu* characters (see subsequent discussion).

setting of the song "Guu Yuann" by Jiang Kwei and the setting of the short song "Kaijyy Hwanging Yn" and the five instrumental pieces "Gong Diaw," "Shang Diaw," "Jyue Diaw," "Jyy Diaw," and "Yeu Diaw" found in *Shyhlin Goangjih*. In order to explain the principles of this particular type of tablature, a brief description of the instrument itself is necessary.

The *chyn* is an oblong wooden box about four feet long, seven inches wide on the average, and two inches thick. Lengthwise over the top of the box are stretched seven strings of varying thickness.[56] One long fixed bridge for all of the strings is on the player's right-hand side. The most common way of playing is to pluck a string near the bridge with the right hand and stop the string with the left hand at various fret positions indicated along the strings. For special rhythmic and melodic figures, as well as for many kinds of subtle nuances, there are various exceptions to this general rule. Each tablature, therefore, consists of three basic elements: the string number, the fret number, and a symbol for the particular manner of execution. Little need be said about the string number in Sonq sources except to note that in his introduction to "Guu Yuann" Jiang Kwei uses the character *dah* 大 (big, main) instead of the character *i* 一 (one) for the first string. In later wood-block editions, *dah* has frequently been confused with *liow* 六 (six), which indicates the sixth string,[57] because of the similarity of the characters.

There are thirteen fret positions indicated on the instrument. Among Sonq sources one of the fullest accounts of these is Ju Shi's, which is briefly outlined as follows.[58] On a string of forty-five inches, the lengths between the bridge and frets numbers 8, 9, 10, 11, 12, and 13 are twenty-seven, thirty, thirty-four,[59] thirty-six,[60] thirty-eight,[61] and forty inches respectively, lengths which correspond to A_1, G_1, F_1, E_1, E_1^{-flat}, and D_1 on a *hwangjong* (C_1) string; frets numbers 5, 6, and 7 are one-half

---

[56] See further details in van Gulik, *Lore of the Chinese Lute*, p. 4, which shows a photograph of a Sonq specimen.

[57] Actually the *Chyangtsuen Tsorngshu* edition of Jiang Kwei's music (see Chap. I) distinguishes the two characters quite carefully. Although either one is musically possible, Yang Inliou tends to change most of the *liow* into *dah* (see notes to transcription in Chap. IV).

[58] "Discourses on the Pitches of the *Chyn*," pp. 30a–b, 32b–33a.

[59] The figures of thirty-four and thirty-eight inches used by Ju Shi are round numbers. More accurately, they should be 33.75 and 37.5 inches.

[60] In two instances the text says thirty-five inches (pp. 30a, 31b), an incorrect statement, because Ju Shi mentions that the other side of the fret is nine inches, which would make the total length of the instrument one inch too short.

[61] See above, note 59.

the distances of frets number 9, 11, and the open string (G, E, C); frets numbers 2, 3, and 4 are one-half the distances of frets numbers 5, 6, and 7 (g, e, c); and fret number 1 is one-half the distance of fret number 4 (c'). In terms of proportion to the total length of the string, the positions for the frets are:

13	12	11	10	9	8	7	6	5	4	3	2	1
8/9	5/6	4/5	3/4	2/3	3/5	1/2	2/5	1/3	1/4	1/5	1/6	1/8

This placement of frets is almost identical with the placement on the present-day instrument, the only difference is in the thirteenth fret, which as far as we know on existing instruments today is always seven eighths of the total length instead of eight ninths.[62] This larger second degree,[63] is not the one actually used, because when the whole tone above the fundamental is needed the player is usually told to stop the string a little to the left of the thirteenth fret, showing that the proportion of the desired note is indeed a little bigger than seven eighths. The symbol for this procedure in the tablature is ⼘, which stands for *hueiway* 徽外 (outside the [thirteenth] fret).[64]

Actually, this kind of adjustment was already necessary in Ju Shi's time. In a later passage in the same chapter he discusses the five basic notes of the scale in relationship to the tuning of the string and fret positions. The passage is somewhat obscure but it is quite specific in pointing out that the note a whole tone above the open string is obtained by stopping the string on the left side beyond the thirteenth fret.[65] In *Shyhlin Goangjih* the symbol ⼘, (for 外), which is explained as an abbreviated character for the expression *hueiway* 徽外, is listed as one of the common symbols for the *chyn* tablature. Ju Shi's comment on this adjustment, which follows his explanation of the orthodox cyclical method of calculating the twelve pitches, is probably still applicable to present-day *chyn* manufacturers: "Today people do not know that this is really also the proper method for calculating the fret positions. Rather, they halve [literally, bend in half] the strings four times and pick out the

---

[62] See chart in Yang's *History*, pp. 168–169.

[63] See, however, Willi Apel, *Harvard Dictionary of Music* (Cambridge, Mass., 1944), p. 136.

[64] In *Guuchyn Cheu Hueybian* (A Repertory of Chyn Music), pp. 38–39, 86f. Many examples of *hueiway* are shown in the tablature and the transcriptions.

[65] "Discourses on the Pitches of the *Chyn*," p. 31b: 且以初絃五音之初言之，則黃鐘之律固起於龍齦而為宮聲之初矣太簇則應於十三徽之左而為商⋯次絃則太簇之律固起於龍齦而為商之初矣而其始角應於十三之左.

central point each time. This is the vulgar method of obtaining the basic units to build up the various proportions. While it may seem to be a simple and easily learned method for obtaining the tones, people do not understand the basis behind these phenomena of nature. It is feared that there are some imperfections."[66] There is not enough information here to show how the entire set of thirteen frets was located by this "halving" method. Nevertheless, the procedure by which the thirteenth fret at the seven-eighths division was obtained is quite obvious.

Besides the position beyond the thirteenth fret, which is indicated by a special symbol for the abbreviated form of [*huei*] *way,* there are many other positions used on the *chyn* today which might be called "fractional positions."[67] To indicate these, the spaces between the frets are each subdivided into ten parts, regardless of whether the space is large or small. Each one tenth of such a space is always called a *fen* 分, and on the tablature the *fen* number is simply written below the fret number. In the following discussion I have also adopted this method of indicating whole and fractional positions with numerals. Many of these fractional numbers are for notes very commonly used. The number 5, 6, for example, stands for the fourth degree an octave above the fundamental, and 7.6 is for the note a minor seventh above the fundamental. A much rarer case is 8.9, found in "Jyue Diaw" in *Shyhlin Goangjih* (see transcription in Chapter IV), which is treated like a kind of ornamental note on fret number 9.

Fractional positions are very frequently used for the adjustment of certain tones; the most common examples are 5.9 for 6, 7.9 for 8, 10.8 for 11, and, as mentioned above, the *way* position for 13. In the Sonq sources some of these fractional positions are the same as those in the present-day tablature, for example 5.6, 7.6, and *way,* which appear in Jiang Kwei's "Guu Yuann," and 10.8 in *Shyhlin Goangjih.* However, there are many cases of 11 in *Shyhlin Goangjih* and "Guu Yuann" (and also of 8 in "Guu Yuann")[68] that remain unmodified. More curious is the

---

[66] Ibid., p. 31a: 今人殊不知此其布徽也，但以四折取中為法，蓋亦下俚立成之小數雖於聲律之應若簡切而易知，但於自然之法，憒不知其所自來則恐不免有未盡耳

[67] In the widely used *chyn* manual *Introduction to the Study of the Chyn* by Jang Heh, I.27b, twenty-six fractional positions are given.

[68] Yang, in his transcription and edited edition of the tablature for present-day players (*Studies,* pp. 81–85), has changed all of the 11 to 10.8 and all of the 8 to 7.9.

use of 8.9 in both sources mentioned above and of 6.9 in "Guu Yuann,"[69] because the ninth and seventh frets, producing the fifth and the octave above the fundamental, are the most accurate frets on the instrument, and are usually relied upon for tuning the strings.

Regarding the tuning of the *chyn,* Ju Shi shows that the standard tuning of the seven strings was C_1, D_1, F_1, G_1, A_1, C, D. He does this by naming the notes at the same position on different strings.[70] It is evident that this pattern of tuning was well established, although the series of notes produced by the open strings differs from the basic pattern of the pentatonic scale, C, D, E, G, A.[71] It is important to note that in referring to the third string, he always calls it the *jyue* 角 string. *Jyue* is usually understood as a major third above *gong* (fa), but when applied to strings here it could only mean "number three."[72] Another source of information on the tuning systems of the Sonq period is Jiang Kwei's partially preserved work *Dahyueh Yih* [Expounding the Great Music], which describes five types of tuning for the seven-stringed *chyn* with the following names.[73]

Gongdiaw	宮調	C_1, D_1, F_1, G_1, A_1, C, D
Mannjyuediaw	慢角調	C_1, D_1, E_1, G_1, A_1, C, D
Chingshangdiaw	清商調	C_1, E_1, F_1, G_1, A_1, C_1, D
Manngongdiaw	慢宮調	C_1, D_1, F_1, G_1, A_1, B_1, D
Rueibindiaw	蕤賓調	C_1, D_1, F_1, G_1, B_1^{-flat}, C, D

The following discussion of the finger technique on the *chyn* is limited to techniques that actually appear in the Sonq music preserved, although many more are found in *chyn* treatises of this period.[74] The various kinds of finger technique found in the music range from specification of the use of certain fingers and the direction from which the string should be struck, like fingering in keyboard music or bowing signs in string

---

[69] In all cases Yang has changed the 8.9 to 9 and 6.9 to 7 (*ibid.*).

[70] His later section dealing specifically with tuning, "Tyau-Shyan" (Tuning the Strings), in which he tries to locate identical notes on different strings, is actually more involved and really adds nothing new.

[71] See pp. 52–53 on Ju Shi's peculiar reasoning in favor of the tuning using an F_1 instead of an E_1.

[72] Jiang Kwei also uses the term *jyue* in this manner. See *mannjyuediaw* below. Note also the extended use of the terms *gong* and *shang* in these cases.

[73] "Mann jyue" obviously means "lowered third string" here; "ching shang," "raised second string"; and "mann gong," "lowered higher octave of first string (or sixth string)."

[74] See Chap. I on Sonq treatises of the *chyn*. The contents of these treatises, quoted ex-

music,[75] to those manipulations that involve distinct rhythmic or melodic modifications, such as the vibrato and the inverted mordent. Descriptions in the Sonq treatises[76] are, on the whole, not difficult to understand, and a majority of the symbols, which are actually abbreviated characters describing the motion of the fingers, are identical with those in present-day manuals.[77] Very few terms have changed their meaning during the intervening centuries.

The subject of rhythm in *chyn* music is somewhat elusive. In the tablature for the *chyn* there are occasional signs (a circle) to show the end of a phrase, or instructions to "slow down," "rest a little," "speed up," but the individual notes have no indication of time value. Since techniques of execution tend to produce definite melodic lines and rhythmic patterns, the characteristics of modern *chyn* playing[78] invite speculation on ancient practices. A *chyn* player today normally still acquires his skill and knowledge through the traditional manner of oral teaching. But by reading the tablature alone a player who is familiar with the general style of *chyn* music can render an unfamiliar work into something plausible to our present-day ears.[79] However, even when the interpretation of small groups of notes are correct there is still the question of the rhythm of a whole phrase.

I have made a cursory survey of some of the techniques in present-day

---

tensively in later works, are gathered in the recent study by Uang Menqshu, *Usylan Manual*. Even the *SLGJ* explains many more symbols than are necessary for reading the seven *chyn* pieces.

[75] This type of differentiation will not be indicated in the transcription in the present study.

[76] Besides making use of some of the Sonq manuals quoted by Uang Menqshu (Chap. I, note 126), I have also included comments of some pre-Sonq works also from his *Usylan* study. These are: *Usylan Guuchwan Chyn Jyyfaa* 烏絲欄古傳琴指法 (The Ancient *Usylan* Manual on the Finger Techniques for the *Chyn*); *Jeantzyh* 減字 (Reduced Characters for the *Chyn*), ascribed to Tsaur Rou 曹柔 (Swei or early Tarng); *Jyyfaa* 指法 (Manual on Finger Technique), ascribed to a certain Chern Shyh 陳士 or Chern Jiushyh 陳居士 (Tarng); and *Jyyfaa* 指法 (Manual on Finger Technique), ascribed to a certain Chern Jwo 陳拙 (end of Tarng).

[77] For example, the standard manual today, Jang Heh's *Introduction to the Study of Chyn* (hereafter *Ruhmen*), which is also much used by van Gulik in his explanations (*Lore of the Chinese Lute*, pp. 120–133).

[78] *A Repertory of Chyn Music* (hereafter *Hueybian*).

[79] This method has been used by *chyn* players today who are trying to reconstruct old *chyn* works preserved only in writing. The method is called *daa-puu* 打譜. The four versions of *Iou Lan* in *Guuchyn Cheu Jyi* (A Collection of Chyn Music) is an example. (On *daa-puu* see *Hueybian*, p. 6, note 1).

practice from transcriptions of actual performances.[80] Certain types of sequential patterns in rhythm and even in the melody, it seems, are created not for an aesthetic reason but merely from a mechanical movement (once or continuous) of the fingers. Some of the extramodal notes in the *chyn* pieces in *Shyhlin Goangjih,* for example, might be explained this way. (See notes to transcription of the *chyn* pieces in *Shyhlin Goangjih* in Chapter IV.)

One general observation should be made before going into the details of finger technique. A technique is usually applied continuously to all of a series of notes if there is no indication of a new technique to cancel the previous one. Therefore, a fret number or the use of a particular finger in a special manner is indicated only on the initial string number, if, in playing the following strings, the same fret or playing technique is used. Sonq sources do not mention this fact as a general rule, but the frequent occurrence of plain string numbers, following a tablature with full instructions, leaves no doubt that such was the convention. Today the practice is simply taken for granted.

Symbols for right-hand technique

1. 乇 for *tuo* 托. "The thumb [nail] pulls the string inward [toward the player]."[81]

2. 尸 for *boh* 擘. "[The fleshy part of] the thumb hooks the string outward [away from the player]." Uang Menqshu (*Usylan,* pp. 7b–8a) notes that the meanings of Number 1 and this symbol have been reversed since the beginning of the Yuan period. Hence this definition from a Sonq source is the opposite of that used at present.[82]

3. 木 for *moo* 抹. "The index finger pulls the string inward."

4. ㇄ or ㇄ for *tiau* 挑. "The index finger hooks the string outward."

5. 勹 for *gou* 勾. "The middle finger pulls the string inward."

6. 丂 for *ti* 剔. "The middle finger hooks the string outward."

7. 丁 for *daa* 打. "The ring finger pulls the string inward."

8. 厂 for *lih* 歷. *Shyhlin Goangjih* gives the fuller form of this symbol without further explanation. Chern Shyh (see above, note 77) of the

---

[80] I have used the transcriptions in *Hueybjan* which are mainly based upon performances by Shiah Ifeng 夏一峯. Wang Guangchyi has also described in staff notation many common fingerings used at the present time, *History,* II.27–39.

[81] The definitions for nos. 1–7 are taken from *SLGJ,* 4.21a–b.

[82] See for example *Ruhmen,* p. 20a–b. However, the *Jyy Hae* edition of *Seh Puu* (I.26), which is from late Sonq or early Yuan, already gives these two definitions in the same order as the later versions.

Tarng describes it as "hooking several strings outward in succession with the index finger" (Uang, p. 7a). The more than forty examples of *lih* in *Hueybian* are all in stepwise descending notes and, with very few exceptions, are all in time values reduced in relationship to the surrounding notes. Most frequently they are reduced by one-half the value of the preceding notes (p. 19. row 1; p. 24, rows 6 and 8; p. 52, row 5; and so forth); those reduced to one quarter are usually in a pattern of ♩.♫♩ (24.3, 29.4, 31.8, and so forth); or in the last two notes of a ♩♪♩ pattern (18.1, 19.8, 34.5, 50.2, and so forth).

9. ㄨ for *jiuan* 蠲. *Shyhlin Goangjih* says, "The index and middle fingers together pull the string inward."[83] The various opinions among *chyn* treatises of Tarng and Sonq (Uang, p. 5a–b) seem to be divided between those that favor the simultaneous movement of the two fingers and those that favor a quick succession of the two fingers on the same string; that is, ♪♩. At present the latter practice is the more common (Jang Heh's *Ruhmen* I. 22a; Yang Yinnliou's *Studies*, p. 83).

10. ㄙ for *jiuan* 涓. The Sonq treatise *Mingshuh Faduan* (Uang, p. 5b) gives the same interpretation as for Number 9 above. Only this form appears in Jiang Kwei's "Guu Yuann," but both forms are found in the music in *Shyhlin Goangjih*.

11. 芴 A combination of Numbers 3 and 5 above, producing two tones which are actually quite similar to a version of Number 9 or 10. In fact, *Ruhmen* (I.22b) considers this one kind of abbreviated symbol for Number 9. But in some practices today the first note seems to have a longer value. Yang transcribes them ♫. (*Hueybian*, 73.8) and ♫ (23.7, 35.4, and so forth). Wang Guangchyi gives the two notes equal time with no special reduction in value (*History*, p. 28).

12. 芎 Combination of Numbers 5 and 6, producing two tones. In most present-day practices these are equal in duration and are without reduction in value (Wang, *History*, p. 26). A few exceptions are the ♩ ♩ and ♪ ♩ rhythm (*Hueybian*, 27.1, 63.1, 67.6, and so forth) and even the ♫ pattern (43.4, 75.1, 84.5, and so forth).

13. 杏 Combination of Numbers 3 and 4, producing two tones. In Wang Guangchyi's description and in by far the more frequent cases in *Hueybian*, these are two even notes and are not reduced in time value. A few exceptions are found in the ♩ ♪ pattern (*Hueybian*, 54.1, 66.6, and so forth) and in the ♪ ♩ pattern (43.3, 68.1, 75.1, 93.1, and so forth).

14. 雴 for *doansuoo* 短鎖. The Sonq treatise *Tarn-chyn Shooushyh Twu*

[83] 蠲也，以食中兩指齊下勾抹.

[83]

弹琴手勢圖 (Uang, p. 9b) says, "On the same string with the index finger first hook the string outward, then pull the string inward, producing two tones. Then repeat and again produce three more tones, altogether producing seven tones. There is another way: first pull inward and hook outward with the index finger, then quickly hook outward with the middle finger and pull in with the index finger, then hook outward with the index finger, thus producing five tones altogether."[84] The pattern given by Wang Guangchyi (p. 28) is ♩ ♩ ♫ ♪. No other *doansuoo* are found in *Hueybian*. In the more recent (1962) collection of *chyn* transcriptions *Guuchyn Cheu Jyi* (which unfortunately I did not have time to incorporate wholly in the present study)[85] there are a few examples of *doansuoo* similar to Wang's figure (*Guuchyn Cheu Jyi* 29.4, 32.6, 58.8), but there are also examples of ♫ ♩ (ibid, 69.5, 70.7).

15. 合 for *luen* 輪. *Shyhlin Goangjih* uses another portion of the character; that is, 冊, and describes the action as follows: "The index, middle, and ring fingers hook the string outward in a connected fashion." Chern Shyh of the Tarng period (Uang, p. 6b) differs from this interpretation in the order of the fingers: first the ring, then the middle, and then the index fingers. *Hueybian* shows that this symbol is nowadays always played in faster notes. Two thirds of the examples are in ♫♫ or ♫♫ rhythm (35.1, 36.2, 46.2, and so forth) and the other third are all real triplets (16.2, 17.2, 54.1, and so forth).

16. 奎 for *chyichuoh* 齊蹴. This symbol appears at the end of three pieces in *Shyhlin Goangjih* and is described in several Sonq treatises (Uang, p. 10a) as a plucking of two strings (which can be from three to six strings apart) with the fingers moving toward each other. The two sounds should not be exactly simultaneous but staggered just a little.

17. 牵 for *chyitsuo* 齊撮. This slight variation of the above symbol appears only at the end of one piece, "Jyue Diaw," in *Shyhlin Goangjih*. According to the same sources it is different in that the two sounds are played simultaneously. Number 16 is used in older music such as "Iou Lan"; in later *chyn* works Number 17 is used exclusively. The appearance of both forms here may show that the *chyn* works in *Shyhlin Goangjih* were written at a transitional period of these two forms.[86]

[84] 先挑抹二聲, 又作二聲, 後又連作三聲, 共七聲, 一説先抹挑, 急剔急抹, 挑, 共五聲.

[85] Compiled by the Institute for the Study of Chinese Music (Peking) as a sequel to *Guuchyn Cheu Hueybian*.

[86] See Wang Shyhshiang's study on this subject, "On the *Chyn* Melody 'Goangling Saan.' "

18. 手 This symbol is not explained in Sonq sources. Yang (*Illustrations of Musical Materials*, p. 82), following Ferng Shoei's 馮水 suggestion, calls it *lei* 雷 (usually 雨), meaning to pluck the seventh, sixth, and fifth open strings in arpeggio. This symbol is not in *Ruhmen* but is explained in another popular Ching manual, *Chyn Music from the Pine-Wind Studio* by Cherng Shyong.[87]

Symbols for left-hand technique

1. ⺌ for *saan*[88] 散, open string. The Sonq monk Tser Chyuan (Uang, p. 12b) explains that no matter what finger or direction the right hand uses, as long as the left hand does not touch the string, the technique is called *saan*.

2. 一, 二, 三, 四, 五, 六, 七, 八, 九, 十, 士, 壵, 壴. These are the numerals 1, 2, 3, 4, 5, 6, 7, 8, 9, 10, 11, 12, and 13 used to indicate the fret numbers and are usually placed on the top right-hand corner of the tablature. The first seven figures are also used in larger woodcut sizes to indicate the string numbers and are usually placed at the lower center part of the tablature.[89] Fractional numbers have been discussed in detail above, but one further note should be added: the symbol 十 stands for .5 when combined with a fret number (for example, 尘 is 9.5). (See Yang, *Studies*, p. 83.) This symbol is not explained in Sonq sources; *Ruhmen* (I.27b) shows that the present-day form for .5 is 夫.

3. 卜 for *hueiway* 徽外. See general discussion on frets of the *chyn*.

4. 大 for *dahjyy* 大指, the thumb.

5. 人 for *shyrjyy* 食指, the index finger.

6. 中 for *jongjyy* 中指, the middle finger.

7. 夕 for *wumingjyy* (無) 名指, the ring finger.

8. 丂 for *yn* 吟. *Shyhlin Goangjih* says, "It can be done with either the fleshy part or the nail of the finger. Move the finger back and forth to extend the sound."[90] On single notes this is similar to the vibrato. In the Sonq examples *yn* is used on two or three successive notes without additional plucking of the string. *Hueybian* shows that this technique can be applied to a long passage (32.2, 74.4 and so forth). It seems, therefore, that the expression "extend" is to be taken literally. The various Sonq sources (Uang, p. 17b) show that *yn* can be combined with many other

---

[87] Introduction, p. 66.

[88] Nos. 1, 3, 4, 5, 6, 7 are listed in *SLGJ* with the fuller equivalents.

[89] In rarer cases the first string is also indicated by the character *dah* 大 "big." See previous discussion on indication of strings.

[90] 有肉吟, 有甲吟, 以指往來, 延其琴韻.

techniques.

9. 犭 for *nau* 猱. Chern Shyh of the Tarng period (Uang, p. 17a) says, "*Nau* is heavy and *yn* is light."[91] Uang (*ibid.*) shows that *nau* 猱 is the same as *now* 獶 or *naw* 臑, which are more common in earlier sources. *Shyhlin Goangjih* has 犭 in the music but the character 臑 in the explanation, and the explanation suggests something more than a vibrato, which is more like Number 25 below: "After plucking the string, move the left hand up a little to produce another note; then return quickly."[92]

10. 來往 *laiwoang*, back and forth. The Sonq sources do not explain this term. *Ruhmen* (I.30a), giving the more condensed form 徠, describes it as moving back and forth between the indicated fret and the upper or sometimes the lower fret. The use of this technique in the Sonq example "Jyue Diaw" (note 3 of transcription) is applied to the very small interval between 8.9 and 9. It could be executed somewhat slower than a regular vibrato.

11. 𢆶 for *chuoh* 綽. *Shyhlin Goangjih* says, "Moving up [to the right] and making the gliding sound seem to begin from nowhere; one should begin at a considerable distance to the left of the intended fret."[93] See Number 19 below.

12. 主下 for *juhshiah* 注下. Only *juh* is explained in *Shyhlin Goangjih*: "Moving downward [to the left] making the gliding sound seem to disappear into nothing; one should begin at a considerable distance to the right of the intended fret."[94] See Number 19 below.

13. 丷 also for *juh* 注, which is more common in later works. Both forms appear in the music of *Shyhlin Goangjih*.

14. 弓上 for *yiinshanq* 引上. *Shyhlin Goangjih*, explaining only *yiin*, says, "After striking the string, move the finger up along the string while pressing firmly so that it is audible."[95] "Guu Yuann" has both 弓上 and 弓下, but the music in *Shyhlin Goangjih* has only the former.

15. 卯下 for *yihshiah* 抑下. This is not explained in *Shyhlin Goangjih*. Chern Jwo of the Tarng (Uang, p. 16b) discusses it under *cherngsheng* 承聲 (sustained sound): "The *cherngsheng* has the *yiin* and the *yih* method ... For example, press the ninth fret [with the left hand] and pull the fifth string [with the right hand]; then move the pressing finger up to the eighth fret. This is called *yiin*. If one presses first the eighth fret while

91 重曰犭, 輕曰ラ.
92 隨所彈絃上少許撞一聲急復.
93 綽, 向上, 使來聲無頭, 遠綽在徽外.
94 注, 向下, 使去聲無頭, 遠注在徽內.
95 打之後, 以按指隨絃緊引上有聲.

pulling the fifth string and then moves the pressing finger downward to the ninth fret, this is called *yih*."[96] In other words, Numbers 14 and 15 are the upward and downward methods of producing the portamento. In the transcriptions, Numbers 11 and 12 will be indicated by arrows preceding the note, and Numbers 14 and 15 by a wavy line between the two notes.

16. 寸 This symbol appears in *Shyhlin Goangjih* in a fuller form: 対 meaning *duey'ann* 對按 which Tzer Chyuan (Uang, p. 16a) says indicates that "the thumb and the ring finger press on two adjacent frets simultaneously." *Duey'ann* is usually associated with *tauchii* (see Number 27 below), but here it is used alone. In the *Shyhlin Goangjih* examples, the symbol always modifies an isolated fret number following a full tablature with a higher fret number. Very likely, this means that after the thumb note is played, the thumb should be lifted without moving the left hand and the ring-finger note played.

17. ㄋ乄上 for *yn'naushanq* 吟猱上. Shift to the right with vibrato.

18. ㄩ In the musical examples this unexplained symbol always occurs at a shifting of the left hand in the right hand direction. It is possibly a kind of vibrato.

19. 上, 下 *shanq, shiah,* literally, up, down. Although these two characters appear separately with fret numbers in the music, they are not discussed in Sonq sources. *Ruhmen* (I.28a–b) explains that moving to the right is "up" and moving to the left is "down." But it does not say how they differ from the symbol for the portamento, the *juh,* and so forth (see above, numbers 12, 14, 15, 17, and so forth).

20. 为 for *budonq* 不動. The Sonq treatise *Tarn-chyn Shooushyh Twu* (Uang, p. 18a) mentions this symbol under *duey'ann* 對按 (Number 27 below). It means "without vibrato or other movements in the left hand," keeping the left hand firmly in position.[97] *Ruhmen* (I.35b) further explains that when the left hand stays firmly on the pressed string, the right hand can proceed to play other strings.[98] In the transcriptions a slur extended beyond the following note is used to indicate the continuation of this note.

21. 尤 for *jiow* 就. This is not explained in Sonq sources. *Ruhmen* (I.35a) says, "Proceed at the same position, or in playing a different

---

[96] 使引按或使抑按…假如按九徽, 抹五絃, 引上八徽名曰引按, 如按八徽抹五絃, 抑下九徽, 名曰抑按.

[97] 對按, 不吟不引曰不動.

[98] 按處不動而彈別絃也.

string, use the same fret."[99]

22. 电 for *yean* 罨. In Tarng and Sonq sources the top part of the character ⼐ is also often used (Yang, *Studies,* p. 82). The Sonq work *Mingshuh Faduan* (Uang, p. 15b) explains: "While the ring finger of the left hand is pressing on the string, the thumb strikes the string."[100] The tone thus produced, of course, depends on the position of the thumb rather than on that of the ring finger.

23. 庵 for *shiuyean* 虛罨. Again, *Mingshuh Faduan* (Uang, p. 15b) says: "With either the thumb, the middle, finger or ring finger of the left hand, knock on the string to produce a tone. This requires no plucking."[101]

24. 內 for *huann* 喚. This symbol is not described in early sources. The description in *Ruhmen* (I.32a) agrees with Wang Guangchyi's figure

(*History*, p. 38). In the *Hueybian* transcriptions, where this symbol appears in the tablature, Yang has simply used a single note (59.1, 2, 3, 4, and so forth). Possibly, as *Ruhmen* (*ibid.*) has pointed out, this symbol also stands for *huann* 換, to change the finger,[102] in which case it has no effect upon the music.

25. 立 for *juanq* 撞. Chern Jwo of Tarng (Uang, p. 18a) mentions this in connection with various kinds of *yn* (above, Number 8). Under *shuenn-yn* 順吟 it says, "This is also called *juanq*. The thumb should be held sideways at the designated fret to sustain the sounding note. Then knock suddenly against the string at the same position again. The weak and loud tones should be distinct. After obtaining this tone, roll back the thumb to the left. In this procedure a definite speed must be observed."[103] In *Hueybian* many examples of *juanq* have a simple repeated note (33.3,7, 41.2,4, 42.1, 83.2,3,5, and so forth); but many also involve a movement upward and back to the original note again. This may be a second above (85.3,6, 87.7) or a third above (45.3,4,5, 51.2,5). In both types a

[99] 就此位弹或弹他絃而徽位同者.
[100] 假如名指按用大指按絃是也.
[101] 或大指或中指, 或名指按絃要有聲, 不必弹
[102] 有以換指按位寫內者.
[103] 順吟, 又名撞, 如使大指側指承聲徽往徽上猛撞, 詳其輕重, 得聲轉指向下, 須知緩急.

dotted rhythm $\sqcap$ $\rfloor$ is most common. Wang Guangchyi gives

as the standard figure (*History*, p. 38).

26. 目 for *daychii* 帶起. Cherng Yuh of Sonq (Uang, p. 14b) gives the form 由 and says: "With the finger on the string, hook up the same string and produce a note."[104] The result of course is the note of the open string.

27. 替 for *duey'ann* 對按 (对) and *tauchii* 搯起 (呂). Only the full characters for *duey'ann* are given in *Shyhlin Goangjih*. *Tarn Chyn Shooushyh Twu* of Sonq (Uang, p. 16a) says that the left-hand thumb first produces a tone by striking the string at the ninth fret, then the ring finger presses upon the tenth fret, then the thumb hooks up the string again.[105] The latter part of this process is *tauchii*. The two tones produced in succession are always one fret apart.

28. 推出 *tueichu*, literally, push out. Chern Shyh of Tarng (Uang, p. 14b) says: "After the string has been plucked, the left-hand middle finger, which has been pressing down the string, quickly moves to the left and then pushes the string out, producing another tone."[106] Cherng Yuh of Sonq (*ibid.*) adds: "This execution is only used by the middle finger on the first string."[107] Thus *tueichu* will always produce the note of the first open string. The initial downward glide is not used in present-day practice (see definition in *Ruhmen*, p. 33b) or in illustrations in *Hueybian* (54.4, 49.3, 55.7, and so forth). But "Yeu Diaw" of *Shyhlin Goangjih* keeps this combination together, as specified by the words *juhshiah* 注下, slide the left hand downward (above, Number 12), just before the expression *tueichu*.

29. ノ for *fannsheng* 泛聲, in harmonics. *Shyhlin Goangjih* gives the form 乏. Many Sonq sources, such as Chern Yang's *Treatise*,[108] also use the character *fann* 汎. Chern Yang describes the procedure: "Touch the string lightly with the left hand while the right hand strikes the string. This produces a thin, clinking sound." "Guu Yuann," which has the

---

[104] 以所按指，惹起現按之絃，令有帶聲是謂帶起.
[150] 左手大名指對按，假如大按九徽，得聲以名按十徽而大搯起謂之對按也.
[106] 既弾之後急以所按中指，抑下徽外推出，令更有一聲也.
[107] 惟中指於大絃用之.
[108] Also cited in Uang, p. 13b: 左微按絃，右手擊絃泠泠然輕清是汎聲也.

entire third section and the end of the fourth section in harmonics, uses only three fret positions: the ninth fret, which produces the octave and a fifth above the fundamental; the tenth fret, which produces the note two octaves above the fundamental; and the seventh fret, which is one octave above.

30. 正 for *fannjyy* 泛止. Chern Shyh of Tarng says this indicates "the end of harmonics section" (Uang, p. 13a).

General instructions

1. 再乍 for *tzay tzuoh* 再作, repeat. *Shyhlin Goangjih* only says that 乍 is 作.

2. 三乍 for *san tzuoh* 三作, obviously means "three times."

3. 从豆再乍 for *tsorng tour tzay tzuoh* 從頭再作, repeat from the beginning. "Guu Yuann" has 欠豆并乍 which is merely a variant. *Shyhlin Goangjih* even explains that 从 is 從.

4. 从コ再乍 for *tsorng* コ *tzay tzuoh* 從コ再作, repeat from the sign コ. This is in "Shang Diaw" of *Shyhlin Goangjih* (at note 2). Examples in *Hueybian* show that nowadays both Numbers 3 and 4 are usually identical repetitions (31.1,2,3, 32.1, 46.3, and so forth). But at 28.3 there is an example of rhythmic variations in the repetition.

(从厂再乍)

5. 省 for *shaoshyi* 少息. *Shyhlin Goangjih* gives no further explanation. *Ruhmen* (I.24b) simply says "rest a little."[109] In *Hueybian* this symbol appears quite frequently on the last note of a phrase, which one would expect to have a longer duration than the preceding notes (25.6, 35.1, 38.3, and so forth). However, it appears even more frequently at places that can only be considered a short rest or break within a phrase of constant beats. The following is an example (p. 25).

省　　　省　　　省

In the following example only by using short rests or breaks at the 省 without prolongation in time can the very lively rhythmic effect be preserved (66.2–3).

[109] 略歇息也.

[90]

Yang Yinnliou in his transcriptions in the *Hueybian* uses many fermatas. Presumably these were decided upon by the actual performances from which he made the transcriptions (43.1, 54.4,5,6, 82.3, and so forth). But there is only one instance in this whole collection of transcriptions where *shaoshyi* appears together with the fermata (37.7). Although Yang does not use rests at all in his transcriptions, the *Hueybian* examples show that *shaoshyi* plays exactly that role.

6. 刍 for *jyi* 急. *Ruhmen* says (I.35a): "Play quickly."[110] Among the *Hueybian* examples this term appears either on a note that follows the previous note quickly (25.1, 3, 5, 49.7, 68.8, and so forth), or a note that begins a quick passage (68.4, 69.2, and so forth). In both cases the most common reduction is to one-half the original value. In many cases *jyi* is indicated on the short note of a dotted rhythm (50.3, 65.7,8, 68.4, and so forth). The Sonq example is combined with the *lih* (above, right hand, Number 8); the two cases in *Hueybian* have the ♩ ♫ (67.6) and ♫♩ (92.8) patterns.

7. 盒 for *ruhmann* 入慢. *Ruhmen* (I.34b) simply says "Play slowly." In the two examples found in *Hueybian*, one is applied to an entire section of a piece (86.5), the other to a long ritardando section near the end of a piece (34.7).

8. 畢 for *bih* 畢, to finish. This is not found in any of the treatises mentioned above. In later works the more common expression is *cheujong* 曲終, the end of the melody, for which the symbol is 奐 (see *Ruhmen*, I.35b). However, the function of *bih* here is self-explanatory.

9. ๐ This small circle, which appears very frequently in the music of *Shyhlin Goangjih*, is not explained in any of the sources so far mentioned. In "Hwanging Yn," the first piece in *Shyhlin Goangjih*, which has a text, all circles coincide with the phrase endings. In the other five pieces, without text, the circles all come at what seem to be reasonable

---

[110] 急弹也.

breaking points in the melody. (Hence, in the transcription a dash across the top line of the staff has been used.) In present-day practices, the circle appears most frequently[111] on the last note of a phrase, which is usually stressed and, at times, is of comparatively longer duration. The following are some examples from *Hueybian* (52.4–5, 53.1–2).

It must be noted that circles are used very sparingly in some pieces (pp. 46, 48, 49, for example), and frequently not at all.[112]

The Liuhleu Notation

The twelve bisyllabic names for the twelve semitones within the octave are as follows.

hwangjong	黃鐘	c	*rueibin*	蕤賓	f-sharp
dahleu	大呂	d-flat	*linjong*	林鐘	g
taytsow	太簇	d	*yitzer*	夷則	a-flat
jyajong	夾鐘	e-flat	*nanleu*	南呂	a
gushean	姑洗	e	*wuyih*	無射	b-flat
jongleu	仲呂	f	*yinqjong*	應鐘	b

---

[111]/ About 10 percent of the circles in the *Hueybian* appear on weak beats, but half of this number occurs in one piece: No. 14, "Leifeng Yiin" 雷風引.

[112] Only six pieces out of the seventeen in the *Hueybian* collection have circles, and none uses them consistently throughout a whole piece.

These twelve pitch names have had a long history.[113] But it is in the Sonq period that we see for the first time, the use of them for writing music. The method here is to use only the first syllable of each name for the basic octave, and a suffix *ching* 清 is added for the notes an octave above. For example, *hwang-ching* 黃清 *dah-ching* 大清, and so forth, as found in Ju Shi's and Jiang Kwei's collections of ceremonial songs. Shyonq Pernglai uses only *hwang* for *hwang-ching*, but since he gives the *gongcheh* equivalent for every piece, there is no ambiguity.

The relative pitch of the twelve semitones, described in terms of the pitch-pipe lengths derived from the cyclical method of calculation, can be found in Sonq treatises by Chern Yang (chap. 101) or Tsay Yuan-dinq. Tsay advocated the inclusion of six extra notes that have the Pythagorean comma[114] (see Table 4) and Chern Yang on the other hand did not approve of any octave notes at all,[115] but these matters did not seem to bother Sonq composers or compilers when they dealt with real music. The three collections of songs written in the *liuhleu* notation all have concordances with the more popular *gongcheh* notation for the guidance of the performing musicians, and the concordances all extend well over an octave.

No other ornamental signs are used with the *liuhleu* notation;[116] the text of the songs in these collections is the only guide to the phrasing of the melodies. How these pieces may have been performed can only be vaguely inferred from the historical records of some actual performances of ritual music. Chern Yang[117] says that in the court performances of his time each beat of the individual bells was followed by three beats on the bells and chimes that are organized in sets.[118] The court musician Yang Jye (eleventh century) complained to the emperor that in the court music each note of the wind and the stringed instruments was

[113] The first mention of these names with their mathematical relationship is in the philosophical work of the third century B.C., *Leu Shyh Chuenchiou* 呂氏春秋 (The Spring and Autumn of Leu Buhwei), chap. 5.

[114] Twenty-four cents higher than c, g, d, a, e, b. See above, Table 3. Although Shyong Pernglai quotes Tsay Yuandinq's sixty modes based upon the scale of eighteen notes, and even occasionally uses the term *biann* 變 for the slightly higher notes in the introduction of *Seh Puu*, he does not use these terms in the music.

[115] See Chap. I.

[116] The characters *jertzyh* 折字, which appear in Jiang Kwei's ceremonial songs, are a special case. See p. 70.

[117] *Yueh Shu*, 124.9a.

[118] The individual bells are *boh-jong* 鑄鐘, and the bells and chimes in sets are *bian-jong* 編鐘 and *bian-chinq* 編磬.

echoed three times by the percussive instruments (that is, the bells and chimes).[119] Jiang Kwei in his proposal for revising the court music (*Dah yueh Yih*) also describes with disapproval the four strokes on the bells for each phrase of ceremonial songs.[120] It seems then that the four-beat group must have been a common feature in the music, although, as we shall see, it did not necessitate a regular four-beat measure.

Yang Jye further complains that there was too much melisma[121] in the vocal part, and that "even when the text had ended, the music still continued."[122] The adding of the melisma to a basic melodic outline could have been an unwritten tradition, originating from popular practices. We know that many musicians in the Sonq court were recruited from among the common people.[123]

Ceremonial songs are still performed in Confucian temples today. The following is a section of a transcription from an actual performance (in 1956) of this type of ceremonial song.[124]

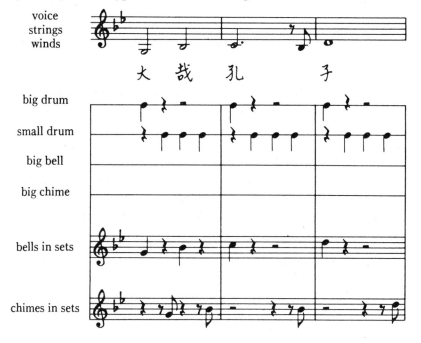

---

[119] *Sonq Hueyyaw*, music section, 5.11; *Wenshiann Tongkao*, 130.7b.

[120] *Sonq History*, 4796b.

[121] *Sonq Hueyyaw*, music section, 5.11; *Tongkao*, 130.7b.

[122] *Ibid.* 或章句已闋,　而樂音未終.

[123] *Sonq Hueyyaw*, music section, 3.16a and 4.8a.

[124] See Yang Yinnliou, "A Preliminary Study of the Spring and Autumn Sacrificial Music in the Confucian Temple," p. 58.

先 覺 先 知

與 天 地 參

The performance was in the County of Liouyang 劉陽 of Hernan Province, where the performance of Confucian rites began only in 1829 under the instigation of the musical scholar Chiou Jyluh 邱之稑, who had much revised the musical arrangement of the songs.[125] Yang Yinnliou, in his study of the ceremonial music, suggests that Chiou's basic rhythmic pattern of ♩ ♩ ♩ ♩ [126] for the four-syllable line must have been a-dopted from one of the more common styles of folksong singing and verse chanting.[127] The alternation of the one and three beats in the percussion group may have been suggested by descriptions in the Sonq sources. But the addition of the extra beat between phrases of course gives it an altogether different rhythmic picture.

In his treatise on ceremonial music[128] Chiou says that the melodic turns in shorter note values are inspired by Ju Shi's statement about interpolated notes. However, Chiou's reference to Ju Shi's work is rather vague. Yang Yinnliou has made a comparison of Chiou's inter-pretation and other collections of ceremonial songs, to show where the extra notes are.[129] They resemble very closely the ornamental notes used in the *kuencheu*, the musical drama current in Chiou's own time.[130]

The Sonq Dynasty Gongcheh Notation

The term *gongcheh*[131] is really borrowed from present-day terminology. There is no specific name mentioned for this set of notational characters in the Sonq sources.

[125] Chiou began his study of ceremonial music at Chiufuh 曲阜, Shantung Province, the home of Confucius, which had been the recognized center of Confucian rites. Chiou's new interpretation, as performed in *Liouyang,* was adopted by Chiufuh later. (Yang, "Sacrificial Music," p. 61.)

[126] *Ibid.* This is also the type of rhythm adopted by Yang in his transcription of the ten ceremonial songs of Jiang Kwei (Yang, *Studies*), but he fits them into the four-beat measures in the following manner: ♩ ♩ ♩ On three-syllable and seven-syllable lines, Yang doubles the last note, a method similarly adopted in his interpretation of Ju Shi's and Shyong Pernglai's ceremonial songs (*Illustrations,* V. 9, 13).

[127] Another common rhythm is the five-beat measure (a pause after the last beat).

[128] See Chiou Jyluh, *Studies on the [Confucian Ceremonial] Music,* preface and chap. 8, section on "General Discussion on the Twelve Classical Songs" (風雅十二詩譜總論), p. 44a–b.

[129] *Spring* and *Autumn Sacrificial Music* p. 63.

[130] Chiou mentions in his preface that he is familiar with the practice of adding ornamental notes in the current popular music. See note 25 above.

[131] *Gong* is the Sixth and *cheh* the fifth of the basic series of the characters used. The name seems obvious enough although we do not know why these particular two notes are chosen for the title.

The entire list as found in Sonq works is as follows:

her	合	c	*shiah-gong*	下工	a-flat
shiah-syh	下四	d-flat	*gong*[133]	工	a
syh	四	d	*shiah-farn*	下凡	b-flat
shiah-i	下一	e-flat	*farn*	凡	b
i	一	e	*liow*	六	c′
shanq	上	f	*shiah-wuu*	下五	d′-flat
gou	勾	f-sharp	*wuu*	五	d′
cheh[132]	尺	g	*jiin-wuu*	緊五	e′-flat

To readers who are familiar with the cursive form of Chinese characters it is not difficult to see the resemblance between these characters and the symbols of the popular notation (see page 59). Similarly, five of them are modified, in this case by the prefix *shiah* to indicate notes a semitone lower than the unmodified characters; and the word *jiin* 緊 (tight) is added to the last symbol *wuu* for the highest note. Sheen Gua, who gives the earliest account of this notation, also uses the prefix *gau* 高 (high) to distinguish the regular notes from the *shiah* notes. But if *shiah* is used consistently, *gau* is superfluous.

The reason for the existence of the *gongcheh* notation in Sonq sources is not clear. Jiang Kwei gives the complete series and refers to it as the "contemporary method of notation" in contrast to the "ancient method of notation" (that is, the *liuhleu* characters).[134] However, Jiang Kwei writes music in all of the notational systems then current in Sonq (that is, the popular notation, the *chyn* tablature, and the *liuhleu* characters) except the *gongcheh* notation. The *gongcheh* notation appears in all major musical sources of Sonq, but practically always for theoretical discussions or general accounts of musical matters (except *Seh Puu;* see below).

Often the *gongcheh* notation seems to be used simply when pitch is referred to. For example, Sheen Gua says: "In tuning the *chyn* today, one must begin by adjusting the first string to the pitch of *her* with the aid of the flute."[135] Jang Yan (*Tsyr Yuan*) and Chern Yuanjinq (*Shyhlin Goangjih*)[136] are even more specific when they distinguish the *gongcheh* notation from the popular notation, by calling the former *goanseh* 管色,

---

[132] This is a special reading today for the musical meaning. The usual current pronunciation is *chyy.*

[133] Not to be confused with the solmization name *gong* 宮 (*fa*).

[134] 古今譜法 *Songs of Whitestone the Taoist,* I.7.

[135] *Memoirs at Menqshi,* par. 111: 如今之調絃，須先用管色合字定宮絃.

[136] I.48, and 5.62a respectively.

[sound on the] wind instruments,[137] and the latter *jyyfaa* 指法, fingering. But as we have seen from the musical examples and modal charts, the popular notation also came to be used like pitch names. So this function of the *gongcheh* notation is not exclusive.

On the whole, one can only say that in the Sonq period the *gongcheh* notation is used by writers when they speak on a theoretical level in a more popular language. They may have sometimes preferred the *gong-cheh* characters to the popular symbols because the former are more readable, and hence tend to remain accurate. So far, Shyong Pernglai is the only man we know in Sonq who uses the *gongcheh* notation in actual music.[138] How typical his case is is difficult to judge.

[137] *SLGJ*, 5.62a, also uses the plain word *in* 音 "sound." For example, 厶音合, 夂音六 (the sound of 厶 is 合, the sound of 夂 is 六).

[138] *Seh Puu*. This is accompanied by *liuhleu* notation as well.

Chapter IV

TRANSCRIPTIONS

Music in the Popular Notation

THE SEVENTEEN *TSYR* SONGS OF JIANG KWEI

1. "Lihshimei Linq" 鬲溪梅令 (Lih River Plum)
2. "Shinqhuatian" 杏花天 (Apricot Blossoms Sky)
3. "Tzueyynshang Sheaupiin" 醉吟商小品 (The Little Drinking Song in Sol)
4. "Yuhmei Linq" 玉梅令 (Jade Plum Blossoms)
5. "Nicharng Jongshiuh Dih'i" 霓裳中序第一 (The First Interlude of the Rainbow Skirt Song)
6. "Yangjou Mann" 揚州慢 (Song of Yangjou)
7. "Charngtyngyuann Mann" 長亭怨慢 (Sorrows of Parting)
8. "Dannhwangleou" 淡黃柳 (The Golden Willow)
9. "Shyrhwushian" 石湖仙 (The Immortal of Stone Lake)
10. "Annshiang" 暗香 (Hidden Fragrance)
11. "Shuyiing" 疏影 (Scattered Shadows)
12. "Shi Horng'i" 惜紅衣 (Love for the Red Dress)
13. "Jyueshaur" 角招 (Melody in La)
14. "Jyyshaur" 徵招 (Melody in Do)
15. "Chioushiau Yn" 秋宵吟 (Autumn Night)
16. "Chiliang Fann" 淒涼犯 (The Lonely *Fann* Melody)
17. "Tsueylou Yn" 翠樓吟 (Green Pavilion)

PRELIMINARY REMARKS

For the basic transcription I have used the *Chyangtsuen Tsorngshu* (*CTTS*) edition of 1913 and have collated it with the *Syhbuh Tsorngkan* (*SBTK*) photographic reproduction of an edition of 1743. The numerous other later editions mentioned in Chapter I, note 152, such as the *Yuyuan Tsorngke* (*YYTK*) and the *Syhbuh Beyyaw* (*SBBY*), mostly incorporate variant readings from the *SBTK* edition and differ only on a few minor points. Differences are found chiefly between the *CTTS,* *SBTK,* and the first Jang edition, which is not available to me but can be inferred from Yang Yinnliou's transcription and notes of 1956. On several doubtful symbols I have adopted or rejected Yang's interpretation simply on musical grounds.

The various interpretations of the corrupted symbols are summarized in Yang's notes; they will not be repeated here unless the present transcription differs from Yang's. In quoting Yang's versions, for the sake of comparison, I have converted his transcriptions into the keys used here. I have also consulted briefly the transcriptions by Chiou, *Tongkao,* and Picken, *Secular Songs.* On the pitches of the problematic notes, their versions agree mostly with Yang. Therefore I shall only discuss the few outstanding discrepancies in their transcriptions.

The musical notes in the transcription are given without time value. The points of articulation in the text will be indicated with the following signs: a bar across all five lines of the staff indicates the end of a stanza; a bar across two lines indicates the end of rhyming line (*yunn* 韻); a bar across one line indicates the end of a nonrhyming line (*jiuh* 句); a comma above the staff indicates a caesura within a line (*dow* 逗).

The textual analysis is based mainly upon that of *The Imperial Register of Tz'u Prosody* of 1715. For the poems that are not listed in this register the analysis given in *Tsyr Pattern Book* by Lin Dahchuen and the punctuated edition of these songs in the *Tsorngshu Jyicherng TSJC* collection were consulted.

In the transcription the ornamental signs for the pauses, deflections, and so forth, are shown directly above the note to which they are attached in the original notation. These are discussed in detail above, Chapter III, but because the interpretations given by Yang Yinnliou are without conclusive proofs (see Chapter III, note 10), the signs are not transcribed in the present study. In order to show how the ornaments might be interpreted, one of Yang's transcriptions (melody Number 1) is given below the corresponding melody in the present transcription. It should be noted that in Yang's transcription, in *Studies,* page 44, the pitch is one whole tone higher than shown here.

The translation of the titles is only for the convenience of the readers; it is free and no attempt is made to interpret terms such as *linq* or *mann* 令 or 慢, which probably suggest formal features. (Picken has made a study of these terms in his *Secular Songs,* p. 132-133. He has also given a complete translation of the song texts.)

1. 鬲溪梅令

re of a-flat

I

好 花 不 與 殢 香 人 浪 㵘 㵘 又 恐

春 風 歸 去 綠 成 陰 玉 鈿 何 處 尋

II

木 蘭 雙 槳 夢 中 雲 小 橫 陳 漫 向

孤 山 山 下 覓 盈 盈 翠 禽 啼 一 春

Yang Inliou's transcription of the same piece

I

II

[101]

2. 杏花天影

sol of b-flat [1]

I

綠 絲 低 拂 鴛 鴦 浦 想 桃
葉 當 時 喚 渡 又 將 愁 眼 與
春 風 待 去 倚 蘭 橈 更 少 駐

II

金 陵 路 鶯 吟 燕 舞 算 潮
水 知 人 最 苦 滿 汀 芳 草 不
成 歸 日 暮 更 移 舟 向 甚 處

3. 醉 吟 商 小 品

sol of e-flat [1]

又 正 是 春 歸 細 柳 暗 黃 千 縷
暮 鴉 啼 處 夢 逐 金 鞍 去

一 点 芳 心 休 訴 琵 琶 解 語

4. 玉 梅 令

re of g

疏 疏 雪 片 散 入 溪 南 苑

春 寒 鎖 旧 家 亭 館 有 玉

梅 幾 樹 背 立 怨 東 風

高 花 未 吐 暗 香 已 遠

公 來 領 略 梅 花 能 劝

花 長 好 願 公 更 健 便 揉

春 為 酒 翦 雪 作 新 詩

挤 一 日 繞 花 千 轉

5. 霓裳中序第一

sol of a-flat

I

亭皋正望極亂落江蓮歸

未得多病却無気力況紈扇

漸疎羅衣初索流光過隙

歎杏梁雙燕如客人何在

一簾淡月彷彿照顏色

II

幽寂亂蛩吟壁動庾信清

愁似織沉思年少浪跡笛裏

關山柳下坊陌墜紅無消息

[104]

漫 暗 水 涓 涓 溜 碧 漂 零 久

而 今 何 意 醉 卧 酒 爐 側

6. 楊州 慢

fa of e-flat

淮 左 名 都 竹 西 佳 處

解 鞍 少 駐 初 程 過 春 風 十 里

盡 薺 麥 青 青 自 胡 馬 窺 江

去 後 廢 池 喬 木 猶 厭 言 兵

漸 黃 昏 清 角 吹 寒 都 在 空 城

杜 郎 俊 賞 算 而 今 重

到 須 驚 縱 豆 蔻 詞 工

青 樓 夢 好 難 賦 深 情 二 十 四

橋 仍 在 波 心 蕩 冷 月 無 聲

念 橋 邊 紅 藥 年 年 知 為 誰 生

7. 長亭怨慢

漸 吹 盡 枝 頭 香 絮

是 處 人 家 綠 深 門 戶

遠浦縈回暮帆零亂向何處

闐人多矣誰得似長亭樹

樹若有情時不會得青青如此

II

日暮望高城不見

只見亂山無數韋郎去也

怎忘得玉郎分付第一是

早早歸來怕紅蕚無人為主

算只有并刀難翦離愁千縷

8. 淡黃柳

空 城 曉 角 吹 入 垂 楊 陌

馬 上 單 衣 寒 惻 惻 看 盡 鵝

黃 嫩 綠 都 是 江 南 舊 相 識

正 岑 寂 明 朝 又 寒 食

強 攜 酒 小 喬 宅 怕 梨 花

落 盡 成 秋 色 燕 燕 飛 來

問 春 何 在 唯 有 池 塘 自 碧

9. 石 湖 仙

sol of b-flat

I

松 江 烟 浦 是 千 古 三 高

游 衍 佳 處 須 信 石 湖 仙

似 鴟 夷 翩 然 引 去 浮 雲

安 在 我 自 愛 綠 香 紅 舞

容 與 看 世 間 幾 度 今 古

II

盧 溝 舊 曾 駐 馬 為 黃 花

閒 吟 秀 句 見 說 胡 兒

也 學 繪 巾 歇 雨 玉 友 金 蕉

玉 人 金 縷 緩 移 箏 柱

聞 好 語 明 年 定 在 槐 府

10. 暗香

fa of a-flat

舊 時 月 色 算 幾 番 照 我

梅 邊 吹 笛 喚 起 玉 人 不 管

清 寒 與 攀 摘 何 遜 而 今 漸 老

都 忘 却 春 風 詞 筆 但 怪 得

竹 外 疏 花 香 冷 入 瑤 席

II

江 國 正 寂 寂 歎 寄 與

路 遙 夜 雪 初 積 翠 樽 易 泣

紅 萼 無 言 耿 相 憶 長 記 曾

攜 手 處 千 樹 壓 西 湖 寒 碧

又 片 片 吹 盡 也 幾 時 見 得

11. 疏影

苔枝綴玉有翠禽小小

枝上同宿客裏相逢

籬角黃昏無言自倚修竹

昭君不慣胡沙遠但暗憶

江南江北想佩環月夜

歸來化作此花幽獨

猶記深宮舊事那人

正睡裏飛近蛾綠莫似春風

不 管 盈 盈 早 與 安 排

金 屋 還 教 一 片 隨 波 去

又 却 怨 玉 龍 哀 曲 等 恁 時

重 覓 幽 香 已 入 小 窗 橫 幅

12. 惜 紅 衣

fa of b-flat

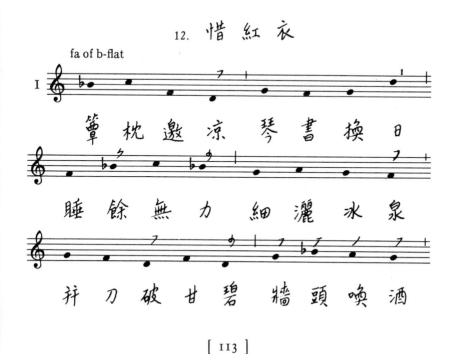

簟 枕 邀 涼 琴 書 換 日

睡 餘 無 力 細 灑 冰 泉

拼 刀 破 甘 碧 牆 頭 喚 酒

誰 問 訊 城 南 詩 客 岑 寂

高 樹 晚 蟬 說 西 風 消 息

虹 梁 水 陌 魚 浪 吹 香

紅 衣 半 狼 籍 維 舟 試 望 故 國

渺 天 北 可 惜 柳 邊 沙 外

不 共 美 人 遊 歷 問 甚 時

同 賦 三 十 六 陂 秋 色

13. 角招

I

為春瘦 何堪更 繞西湖

盡是垂柳 自看煙外岫

記得與君 湖上攜手

君歸未久 早亂落香紅千畝

一葉凌波縹緲 過三十

六離宮遣遊人回首

II

猶有 畫船障袖

青樓倚扇 相映人爭秀

[115]

翠 翹 光 欲 溜 愛 着 宮 黃 而

今 時 候 傷 春 似 舊 蕩 一 點

春 心 如 酒 寫 入 吳 絲 自 奏

問 誰 識 曲 中 心 花 前 友

14. 徵 招

do of c [1]

I

潮 回 却 過 西 陵 浦

扁 舟 僅 容 居 士 去 得

幾 何 時 黍 離 離 如 此

客 遊 今 倦 矣 漫 贏 得

一　襟　詩　思　記　憶　江　南

落　帆　沙　際　此　行　還　是

迤　邐　剡　中　山　重　相　見

依　依　故　人　情　味　似　怨

不　來　遊　擁　愁　鬢　十　二

一　丘　聊　復　爾　也　孤　負

幼　輿　高　志　水　葓　晚

漠　漠　搖　烟　奈　未　成　歸　計

15. 秋宵吟

sol of b-flat

古簾空墜月皎，

坐久西窗人悄蛩吟苦

漸漏水丁丁箭壺催曉

引涼颸動翠葆露腳

斜飛雲表因嗟念

似去國情怀暮帆烟草

帶眼銷磨為近日

愁多頓老衛娘何在

宋 玉 歸 來 兩 地 暗 縈 繞

搖 落 江 楓 早 嫩 約 無 憑

幽 夢 又 杳 但 盈 盈 淚 灑

單 衣 今 夕 何 夕 恨 未 了

16. 淒 涼 犯

re of a-flat [1]

綠 楊 巷 陌 秋 風 起 邊

成 一 片 離 索 馬 嘶 漸 遠

人 歸 甚 處 戍 樓 吹 角

情懷正惡更衰草寒

烟淡薄似當時將軍

部曲迤邐度沙漠

追念西湖上小舫攜歌

晚花行樂舊遊在否想如

今翠凋紅落漫寫羊裙

等新雁來時繫着怕匆

匆不肯寄與悵後約

17. 翠樓吟

sol of e-flat

月 冷 龍 沙 塵 清 虎 落

今 年 漢 酺 初 賜 新 翻 胡

部 曲 聽 韉 幕 元 戎 歌 吹

層 樓 高 峙 看 檻 曲 縈 紅

簷 牙 飛 翠 人 姝 麗

粉 香 吹 下 夜 寒 風 細

[121]

此地宜有詞仙擁素雲

黃鶴與君遊戲玉梯凝

望久歎芳草萋萋千里

天涯情味仗酒祓清愁

花銷英氣西山外

晚來還捲一簾秋霽

TRANSCRIPTIONS

Number 1

1. Yang Yinnliou interprets the two symbols, which are actually different, both as d′; but according to Sheen Gua's table of modes (above Table 3), which in this case is also confirmed by the analysis in Chapter III, they both should be e′-flat.

Number 2

1. The mode of melody Number 2 is probably omitted by accident. Since the final note of this piece is *liow* (c′), Sheen Gua's table of modes shows three possibilities: fa of c, sol of b-flat, or re of e-flat. The analysis of the piece and the rhyme endings show a preference for the intervals of the fourth below and the second above the final (see Chapter III; the sol mode therefore is the most logical choice.

The sixteenth-century anthology of song texts *Jiowbian Nan Jeougong Puu* 舊編南亢宮譜 by Jeang Shiaw 蔣孝 (chap. VI, under *Yiin Tzyy* 引子) lists this song under *yuehdiaw* 越調 (sol of b-flat). A better edition may have been available to the compiler. In more recent times, Jang Wenhuu (pp. 5b–6a) and Yang Yinnliou (*Studies*, p. 32) have chosen re of e-flat.

2. For *cheh* (g), Yang reads *her* (c).

3. The complicated symbol 彡 is read *wuu* (d′); Yang reads *jiin-wuu* (e′-flat).

4. Yang has emended the *shiah-farn* (b-flat) to *wuu* (d′), in order to match the *wuu* in the second stanza.

5. The symbol in the first stanza is 㐄 and in the second stanza ㇀, both of which I read *i—*(e) with an ornamental sign 与; Yang reads both as *gou* < (f-sharp), with the same ornament.

6. *CTTS* agrees with Yang's reading, although *SBTK* and *YYTK* have *liow, cheh* (e′, g), which has been adopted by Chiou.

7. *CTTS* agrees with Yang, but the other editions have *wuu* (d′).

Number 3

1. In this case the modal name is merged with the tune title, which contains the word *shang* 商 (sol). Since the cadencing note is f, the mode is sol of e-flat.

2. For unknown reasons the first character of the text is omitted in the version in the *Imperial Register* (2.1b). The incomplete symbol ∠ I read as *her* 厶 (c); Yang considers it *shanq* 厶 (f), Chiou reads it *cheh* (g).

3. I read the incomplete form ∠ as *her* (c); Yang reads it *gou* < (f-sharp).

Number 4

1. The symbols at these two places appear to be *shanq* ⼑ (f), which is a note outside of the scale of this mode. I am simply following Yang's corrections here.

Number 5

1. The incomplete sign ∠ *shanq* (f), as suggested by Yang.

2. ⼵ looks like a corrupted form of *shanq* ⼑ (f); *SBTK* and *YYTK* editions have a more distinct *liow* ⼍ (c'), which is also preferred by Yang.

3. The symbol which I read *shiah-farn* (b-flat) is read *shiah-gong* (a-flat) by Yang.

4. The next twelve notes occur in several variant forms in the sources. The *SBTK, YYTK, SBBY,* and *TSJC* editions have the following reading.

I have followed Yang's suggestion in adopting the Jang version, while the version in *CTTS* seems a mixture of these two early versions.

5. For *shiah-gong* ⼆ (a-flat), Yang reads *shiah-i* — (e-flat with a sign ⼃).

Number 6

1. Yang uses d' for these two cases.

2. The Symbols at these two places are slightly corrupt. Chiou reads both a.

3. The e-flat and the following a (a combination occurring four times in this piece) form a tritone. In order to avoid this interval Yang has raised the e-flat to e each time. This adjustment, however, upsets the

mode, because e-flat is the final and main cadencing note of the piece. Western theorists in the Middle Ages tried to avoid tritones, but there is no justification for avoiding them here: neither a term for a tritone nor the concept of it appear in the Sonq works. Furthermore, in each case the a in the e-flat, *a, g* figure may be considered a cambiata resolving to g (see Chapter III, p. 65). The f in the beginning of the second stanza may even be considered an unresolved cambiata.

Number 7

1. Yang again raises the e-flat to e to avoid the tritone (see note 2 to the previous melody).

2. For *shiah-i* (e-flat) Yang reads *gong* (a).

3. For 夕 半 夕 which I read *cheh-shanq-cheh* (g, f, g) with ornaments, Yang reads *liow-gong-cheh* (c', a, g) with ornaments. Chiou reads g, b, g.

Number 8

1. For *syh* (d), Yang reads *gong* (a).

2. Yang has lowered this note to b-flat to avoid the tritone. Like the a's in melodies 6 and 7, the b's in this piece in the f, b, a figures also may be considered cambiatas; in the b, c' figures the b's are like appoggiaturas.

3. The incomplete symbol 乄 I read *gong* (a); Yang reads it *farn* (b), and Chiou, *liow* (c).

4. The *SBTK* and *YYTK* editions have an ornamental symbol ✓ on this note.

Number 9

1. The incomplete symbol ∠ I read *her* (c); Yang reads it *shanq* (f), for the sake of a better melodic line (*Studies*, p. 34).

2. Chiou reads this *i* (e).

3. The ornamental symbol in *SBTK* and *YYTK* is ✓ instead.

Number 10

1. *SBTK* has *liow* (c') here.

2. Yang uses d'.

Number 11

1. Yang uses d'. However, while he also uses e-flat in this piece, Chiou uses d' throughout.

2. For the symbol *shanq* (f), Yang reads *liow* (c').

3. The two obscure symbols ㅎ ㅿ I read *syh-her* (d, c) here; Yang prefers to read them as *wuu-liow* (d', c'), in order to match the corresponding place in the first stanza. Actually, by reference to the previous melody (Number 10), which is very closely related to this piece, either reading is possible.

Number 12

1. For the symbol ㅎ, which I read d' here, Yang reads *i* — with an ornamental symbol ㅎ and lowers the e to e-flat.

2. In these three cases Yang reads the symbol ㅎ as e-flat. His reason for the use of flats is not apparent, except perhaps in one case to avoid a tritone.

3. For *shanq* (f), Yang reads *liow* (c').

Number 13

1. The mode used in this piece, la of c, is not one of the twenty-eight popular modes. According to Jiang Kwei's introduction the names "Jyueshaur" and "Jyyshaur" (Number 14) existed during the Jenqher 政和 era (1111–1118), when the musical institute Dahshenq Fuu was flourishing, but these two compositions are his own.

2. The six notes in this phrase have seven characters in the text. The *CTTS* edition simply leaves a blank at the character *shi* 西; the *YYTK* and *TSJC* editions have shifted the last five notes back one to fill the blank space shown here and added an extra e at the word *leou* 柳; the *SBTK* edition stretches the spacing of the last few notes in the phrase, which of course produces additional ambiguous notes. For other attempts to solve this problem, see Yang's notes (*Studies*, p. 35). The interpretation of this phrase is further complicated by the fact that the standard pattern of this poem, given in the *Imperial Register* (34. 27b), actually calls for only six characters in this phrase. The poem quoted by the *Imperial Register* is not the one by Jiang Kwei, but another by Jaw Yiifu 趙以夫 (1189–1256), a younger contemporary of Jiang, who states that he was modeling his poem after Jiang's. Later compilations of *tsyr* patterns containing this poem, such as Lin's *The Tsyr Pattern Book* (pp. 492–493), have omitted the character *shi*, leaving the poetic line still perfectly readable (*hwu* 湖, lake, instead of *shi hwu* 西湖, the west lake); in this reading the melody agrees exactly with that in the second stanza. However, Yang argues that the character *shi* was originally

intended because Jiang Kwei had specifically mentioned "west lake" in his introduction to this song. Therefore, Yang has also chosen to add an extra note (e) to this phrase, but prefers to place it next to the character *shyh* 是 in the text. Chiou solves the problem by omitting *shyh*. The justification for this is that the phrasing thus corresponds better with the next stanza.

3. For the incomplete symbol ∠, which I read f-sharp here, Yang reads c.

Number 14

1. On the mode of this piece, see note 1 of the previous melody.

Number 15

1. I read the symbol for this note *Shanq* (f); Yang reads it *Shiah-farn* (b-flat). *CTTS* has ㇂; *SBTK* has *shanq*.

2. Yang's version has an extra note, g (with an extra character *ann* 暗 in the text), so that his transcription reads as follows.

This may have been the version in the early Jang edition used by Yang. However, in the other versions the note g and the character 暗 do not exist; and the character *yean* 眼 appears with the b-flat.

Number 16

1. The *CTTS* edition does not mention a mode for melody Number 16. The other editions and the *Imperial Register* all contain the statement 仙呂調犯商調 (re of a-flat, making a *fann* into sol of a-flat).

In his preface to this song Jiang Kwei explains the technical term *fann*: "In speaking of *fann* in a song, there are such expressions as 'fa making a *fann* into sol,' 'sol making a fann into fa,' and so forth. For example, a fa of f ends on f, and a sol of e-flat also ends on f. Because they end on the same note, in a fa of f melody, one can make the *fann* into sol of e-flat; or in a sol of e-flat melody, one can make the *fann* into fa of f. Other *fann* can follow this as an example. (凡曲言犯者謂以宮犯商商犯宮之類如道調宮上字住雙調亦上字住所住字同故道調曲中犯雙調或雙調曲中犯道調其他準此)

This description suggests that *fann* means a modulation of parallel keys, that is, alteration of the interval pattern of the scale while keeping the same final cadencing note.

Since the present melody ends on f, the possibilities are re of a-flat, sol of e-flat, and fa of f. Of these, re of a-flat and sol of e-flat are the closest pair, which differ only in the a-flat and a. This is the pair of modes adopted by Yang and Chiou.

The melodic analysis of this piece shows that the interval patterns are closest to that of the re modes. The only hint of a sol mode is that it has a secondary cadence on the second degree above the final, a characteristic of sol melodies. (See above, Table 6.) Both re and sol modes have secondary cadences on the fifth degree above.

However, another outstanding feature in this piece is the borrowing of melodic phrases from other pieces in a different mode, in this case, from fa of a-flat (melodies 10 and 11). This is unusual, because from the table of related melodies of Jiang Kwei (See Chapter I) we have seen that many modes are associated with certain established melodic phrases, and among Jiang Kwei's compositions at least melodies in the same mode tend to share common materials. In a few cases the re modes (X and 1) and sol modes (9 and 17) in different scales also have common passages. But Number 16, the melody under discussion, is the only case where a re mode melody borrows material from fa mode melodies. (Numbers 13 and 14 in la and do modes respectively also share common melodic lines, but, being in theoretical modes, these are exceptions; see notes to these transcription.)

It is true that the expression 仙呂調犯商調, "re of a-flat making an intrusion (*fann*) on sol of a-flat," properly accounts for the one second degree cadencing in this piece of music, but an even better reading would be 仙呂調犯宮調, "re of a-flat borrowing materials from the fa mode," the so-called fa mode being fa of a-flat, or *shianleugong* 仙呂宮 in the popular nomenclature. This reading requires one to change the character *shang* 商 to *gong* 宮; on the other hand, it describes the nature of the *fann* melody more adequately. Picken, also noting the fa mode quality of the melody, has however transcribed the piece entirely in sol of e-flat.

Jiang Kwei's explanation of use of parallel keys which I have not adopted in the transcription deserves serious consideration. That such a technical term needs detailed explanation in the preface to the song shows it could have had a special interpretation under the circumstances.

The trouble with the parallel key interpretation is that we do not know when one mode ends and the other begins. Yang (*Studies,* p. 65) and Chiou (p. 113), both adopting the parallel key scheme, have chosen entirely different sections of the melody for the transition. The results, in both cases, are very awkward.

2. Yang uses d′ here. In this piece Yang and Chiou use both d and e-flat—though not all at the same places, while Picken uses d throughout.

3. For the sake of matching with the second stanza Yang has changed this note to c.

4. For *shiah-gong* (a-flat) Yang reads *syh* (d).

5. The symbol ㇗ which I read *d,* Yang reads *Shiah-i* ㇆ (e-flat).

Number 17

As an example, the entire notation (in the *CTTS* version) is given here above the text.

1. The *SBTK* edition has *shanq* (f), which agrees with the second stanza, but the *CTTS* version has *shiah-farn* (b-flat), which Yang follows.

2. I read the symbol ㇉ as *shiah-farn* (b-flat); Yang reads *gong* (a).

3. For the following five notes Yang mentions that he has followed the editing by Chiou Chyongsuen 丘瓊蓀, 1953 (see Yang, *Studies,* pp. 4, 37), in which Chiou renders the passage c, d, g, f, e-flat, to make it match with the previous stanza. Presumably then, all editions contain the unmatched phrase. Unless this variation is intentional, which is stylistically possible, the mistake probably originated in Taur Tzongyi's manuscript of the Yuan dynasty.

THE SEVEN MELODIES IN *SHYHLIN GOANGJIH* (under the general title of *Yuann Cherng Shuang* 願成雙)

1. "Yuann Cherng Shuang Linq" 願成雙令 (Two with you, Linq)
2. "Yuann Cherng Shuang Mann" 願成雙慢 (Two with You, Mann)
3. "Shytzyy Shiuh" 獅子序 (The Lion)
4. "Beengong Poh Tzyy" 本宮破子 (Piece in the Same key [?])
5. "Juann" 賺 (A Turn [?])
6. "Shuangshenq Tzyy Jyi" 霋勝子急 (The Double Victory)
7. "San Jiuh'erl" 三句兒 (Three Little Lines)

SONQ DYNASTY MUSICAL SOURCES

This transcription is based upon the Yuan edition printed during the reign of Jyhshuenn (1330–1333) which I have collated with the 1699 Japanese edition and the 1418 edition.

The time value will not be indicated. The symbol ╱ , as discussed in Chapter III, seems to suggest a kind of hold or rest; therefore, wherever this symbol appears in the music a bar is placed across the top line of the staff to show some kind of melodic punctuation. The characters *huanntour* 換頭, *wang shiah* 王下, and so forth, which indicate the form of the melodies (see Chapter III), are given in translation at the same place in the music as in the original woodcut. The circles that appear in the music are also indicated at the same places in the transcription.

These melodies present an interesting point about modes. Above the main title, *Yuann Cherng Shuang,* appears the statement, "The name of the mode is *hwang jong-gong* 律名黃鐘宮," and just below this in smaller characters, "Popularly called *jenqgong* 俗呼正宮." The concordances of the popular and classical modal names in all Sonq sources confirm that *hwang jong-gong* here must be the classical modal name (fa of c). In terms of the popular notation, the symbols used ought to be *her* (c), *syh* (d), *i* (e), *gou* (f-sharp), *cheh* (g), *gong* (a), *farn* (b), *liow* (c′), *wuu* (d′). However, the list of symbols appearing in *Yuann Cherng Shuang* differs from this list in having the *shanq* (f) instead of the *gou* (f-sharp), which makes the scale a do scale instead of a fa scale. The *shanq* is one of the symbols with no alternative readings, and its frequency in the music shows that it could not have been the result of scribal errors. A possible explanation for this is that at the time when this music was written, though in theory the basic scale was a fa scale, in practice it was a do scale. This discrepancy occurs also in some of the *chyn* pieces in *Shyhlin Goangjih* (see notes to transcriptions below) where the melodies in the re, fa and sol modes all seem to have one flat too many according to theory. (Number 1, being pentatonic, is ambiguous. Numbers 4 and 5 are modally obscure and have labels of modes not currently in use. See Numbers 2, 3, and 6.)

1. 願 成 雙 令

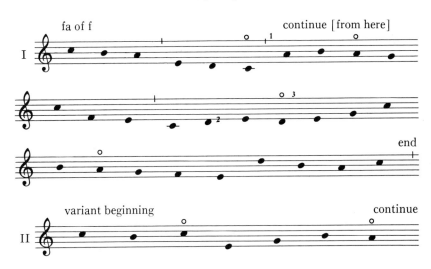

2. 願 成 雙 慢

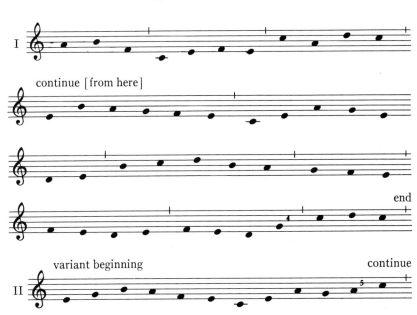

3. 獅子序

continue [from here]

end 9   repeat

continue

the third time

4. 本宮破子

continue [from here]

I

end

o 12

11

variant beginning   continue

II

5. 賺

continue [from
here]

中斗

I

variant beginning   continue

II

6. 靈勝子急

end repeat

7. 三句兒

NOTES TO TRANSCRIPTIONS

1. The pause sign in the 1699 reprint edition is not complete.
2. For *syh* (d) the 1418 edition has *gong* (a).
3. The 1699 reprint has no circle.
4. For *cheh* (g) the 1699 reprint has *her* (c).
5. This note is omitted in the 1699 reprint.
6. For *gong* ㇱ (a) the 1699 reprint has ㇷ, which looks more like a *liow* 仒 (c').
7. The 1418 edition has for this note an obscure symbol, ㇡.
8. The 1418 edition has *cheh* (g).
9. The reason for placing the word *woei* 尾 (end) before the last two notes d', c' (in all editions) is not clear. The last two notes seem to belong to the melody since they balance with an earlier part of the melody in which there is a repeated two-note phrase f, e.
10. The 1418 edition has a repeated *cheh* (g); the other two editions have *her* (c).
11. For *gong* (a) the 1699 reprint has only a pause sign.
12. Only the 1418 edition has a circle here.
13. The 1418 edition has an extra note *i* (e) before the g.
14. This pause sign is missing in the 1699 reprint, leaving a blank space in the music.
15. For *liow* (c') the 1699 reprint has *cheh* (g).
16. For *cheh* (g) the 1699 reprint has *shanq* (f).
17. For *shanq* (f), the 1699 reprint has *liow* (c').
18. For the two notes *i-syh* (e, d) the 1699 reprint has only one note *liow* (c').
19. The 1418 edition has two distorted symbols, ㇌ㄣ, for these two notes, b, a.
20. The pause sign is omitted in the 1699 reprint.
21. The 1418 edition has *shanq* (f).
22. The Jyhshuenn edition has *farn* (b).

THREE PIECES FROM *YUEHFUU HWENCHERNG*

1. "Shiausheng Puu" 嘹聲譜 (Introduction)
2. "Sheaupiin Puu" 小品譜 (A Little Piece)
3. "Yow" 又 (Another Example)

TRANSCRIPTIONS

PRELIMINARY REMARKS

The present transcription is based on a microfilm of the Ming edition of *Cheu Liuh* 曲律 now preserved in the Palace Museum in Taiwan (see Chapter I, note 168). The mode given for these melodies is *linjong-shang* 林鐘商, sol of g, and there is also the statement, "called *shiejyydiaw* during the Swei period [early seventh century]" (隋呼歕指調). This mode, according to Sheen Gua's description (Table 3), is d, e, f-sharp, g, a, b, d', with the final cadence on a. The first piece has only five notes, which make up the pentatonic scale of e, f-sharp, a, b, d'. This seems really a kind of instrumental introduction given simply to establish the mode.

At the end of all three pieces is the symbol ⁄ , which has been assumed throughout to be for melodic punctuation. (Tarng Lan considers it a sign for the note an octave higher.) In Number 3 the symbol also appears at the end of the two rhyming phrases. In all cases the sign is indicated by a short bar in the transcription. The lines of the text are marked by a comma above the staff.

The rhyme scheme of the text of Number 2 is aabb; that of Number 3 is abcaa.

1. 娟聲譜

2. 小品譜

正 天 氣 淒 涼 鳴 幽 砌 向

枕 畔 偏 惱 愁 心 盡 夜 苦 吟

3. 又

戴 花 斟 酒 酒 泛 金 尊

花 枝 滿 帽 笑 歌 醉

拍 手 戴 花 斟 酒

1. Tarng Lan makes this note an octave higher.

2. The symbol for this note appears somewhat different from the symbol for the following note.

3. For the symbol 곡, which I read *farn* (b), Tarng reads *cheh* an octave above (g'). Because of the nature of the scale suggested by the introductory piece, I have attempted to preserve the pentatonic scale when dealing with ambiguous notes in melodies 2 and 3.

4. For the symbol 勹, which I read *gong* (a), Tarng reads *farn* (b).

5. For the symbol 圴, which I read *farn* (b), Tarng reads *cheh* an octave above (g').

6. Tarng reads this an octave higher.

7. For 勾, which I read *wuu* (d'), Tarng reads c-sharp. However, see note 3 above.

8. For 곡, which I read *farn* (b), Tarng reads *gong* (a).

Music in The Chyn Tablature

SIX PIECES FROM *SHYHLIN GOANGJIH*

1. "Kaijyy Hwanging Yn" 開指黃鶯吟 (An Introduction: Song of the Golden Oriole)
2. "Gong Diaw" 宮調 (The Fa Mode [?])
3. "Shang Diaw" 商調 (The Sol Mode [?])
4. "Jyue Diaw" 角調 (The La Mode [?])
5. "Jyy Diaw" 徵調 (The Do Mode [?])
6. "Yeu Diaw" 羽調 (The Re Mode [?])

The transcription of melodies 2–6 is based on the Yuan edition of *Shyhlin Goangjih* now kept in Taiwan (on editions, see Chapter I). I have compared it with the Jyhyuan edition in the Imperial Household Library in Tokyo and the Ming edition of 1418. For melody Number 1 I have used the 1699 edition, which contains just this one piece.

No tuning is given for these pieces. If we assume that the basic tuning of C_1, D_1, F_1, G_1, A_1, C, D was used, the first piece seems designed especially to test the tuning of the strings, because all the repeated notes are played first on an open string and then on a stopped string. The following scheme of the melody shows how all seven strings are checked in this manner. The Roman numerals in this representation refer to the string numbers and the Arabic numerals to the fret numbers. Roman numerals by themselves indicate open strings; the hyphen shows the pairs of repeated notes.

VII-IV$_9$ VI-III$_9$ VII V-II$_9$ VI I IV III-I$_{10}$ II V VI I IV III-I$_{10}$ III VI III-I$_{10}$

Hwanging Yn may have been the name of an existing melody adapted for this purpose. *Kaijyy*, literally, "to commence operation with the fingers," clearly shows the nature of this piece.

In these transcriptions the notes are not given a precise time value, but certain ornamental notes such as those occurring in the *jiuan* 犮 (see page 83) or *huann* 丙 (see page 88) are indicated in notes of lesser value,

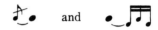

respectively, because the nature of the execution suggests that a quicker tempo for these notes is more appropriate. Where there is a small circle in the tablature, indicating the end of a phrase, I have used a bar across the first line of the staff. The short wiggly sign above a note indicates the *yn,* the vibrato, and the long wiggly sign between notes indicates a portamento. An arrow preceding a note shows the initial upward or downward glide (see page 86). A note with a slur that extends beyond the following note means that it should still sound while the following note is played (see page 87). A small cross indicates a slightly higher pitch than the written note (see discussion on fractional positions on the *chyn* in Chapter III), not the 24 cents as in Table 4.

1. 開 指 黃 鶯 吟

2. 宮 調[1]

3. 商　調[1]

4. 角調[1]

5. 徵調[1]

6. 羽調[1]

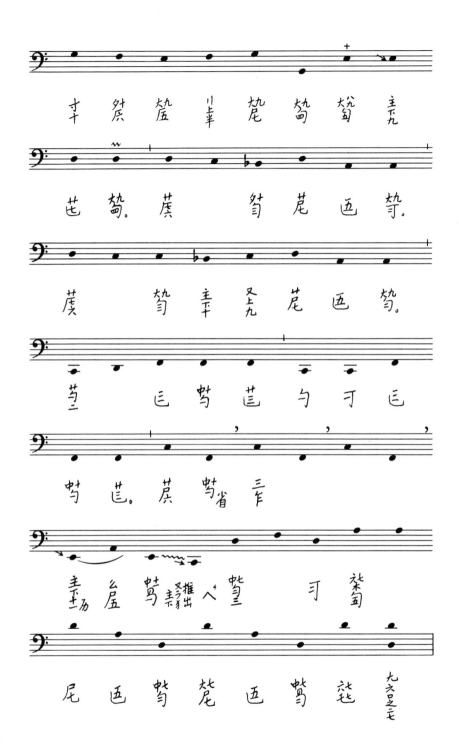

SONQ DYNASTY MUSICAL SOURCES

Number 1

1. Although the Yuan and Ming editions all have 蕤 VI_0 (C), and only the 1699 edition has 蕤 VII_0-VI_0 (D, C), the latter is preferable because the text here has two syllables.

2. The Yuan and the Ming editions have 二, II (D_1), but the 1699 edition has 三, III (F_1). The latter is preferable, first because it agrees with the previous phrase, and second because the *lih* 歷 method (see page 82) is played only on adjacent strings. Leaping from the fourth string to the second string would not be fitting here.

Number 2

1. The title "Gong Diaw" suggests that this is in a fa mode. However, the pentatonic nature of the melody leaves the scale ambiguous: it can be either a fa pattern or a do pattern.

2. I read this symbol *yn* ㇆, vibrato, Thus 圭 means, left hand in vibrato moving up to the tenth fret (in this case, F_1).

3. In all editions the symbol here is incomplete: the Yuan editions have 芍 and the Ming edition has 芎. Since F_1 is the logical cadencing note, the tablature could have been 芍 (I_{10}).

Number 3

1. The title means "the sol mode," but the numerous occurrences of the B-flat makes it really a re mode.

2. This position, $VI_{7\ 8}$, is uncommon today. Fret number 8 would be A_1, and 7.6 would be B_1-flat.

3. This is the sign indicating where the repeat begins.

4. The Ming edition has ㇓ and 刀 here, but the Yuan editions all have 刘, which looks like an abbreviation of *yih* 抑, "to press or push slightly to the left" resulting in a small downward glide.

5. The symbol 㞫 is probably 主, an abbreviation of 注 (see page 86).

6. The Ming edition has *huann* 內 here, but the Yuan editions have *yn* ㇆.

Number 4

1. The title of the piece means "the la mode," and the initial emphasis on A seems fitting. Even the emphasis on D, the fourth degree above the final, agrees with the analysis for the melody in la by Jiang Kwei (see Table 5, number 13). The B_1-flat however, gives the melody

a very different character; furthermore, the cadencing gradually shifts to G.

2. I take this to be *doansuoo* 短鎖 (see page 83) on the third string at the sixth fret.

3. This looks somewhat like 㠯 for *fannchii* 泛起 (to begin playing in harmonics) but the technique given for the subsequent notes cannot be played in harmonics. Reading it *ruhmann* (play in a slower tempo) is a possibility.

4. This means a broader kind of vibrato (see page 86).

5. The meaning of the symbol 少 is uncertain.

6. The symbol 朩 is probably 大, 10.8 (actually the eleventh fret).

Number 5

1. The title means "the do mode." If this key is assumed in this piece, there should be emphasis on C. Instead the tonal center wanders between D, A, and G.

2. The Yuan editions have 𤫩, which is difficult to decipher. The Ming edition has 柔, "vibrato and move to the eighth, then the eleventh, and back to the eighth fret" (that is, F, C-Sharp, F).

3. The Ming edition has fret Number 9 instead of 9.5 for these two notes, in which case the pitches would be C, D.

Number 6

1. The title of the piece means "the re mode." However, the piece is clearly in a la mode because of the B-flat.

2. The Yuan edition in the Imperial Household Library at Tokyo has $III_0(F_1)$, which is probably wrong.

3. The symbol 厶 in 舀 is obscure.

4. This symbol may have been for *ruhmann,* indicating that the following is a ritardando section.

THE SONG "GUU YUANN" BY JIANG KWEI

PRELIMINARY REMARKS

For the basic transcription I have used the *CTTS* edition comparing it with the *SBTK* edition. As I have not had access to the early Jang edition on which Yang based his transcription, I have pointed out in detail differences between his and my transcription in the notes.

Before Yang's transcription of 1956 there had been attempts at transcription by Day Charnggeng in 1833 and Ferng Shoei in 1924 (see Chapter I, note 150), but both contain serious defects. The missing tablatures in the Luh (*SBTK*) edition resulted in a shifting of the alignment of the text with the music at the end of section one and throughout section four in both transcriptions. Furthermore, Ferng Shoei used a different tuning system, making his transcription entirely wrong. Since Yang has discussed these two works extensively (*Studies,* pp. 79–81) they will not be dealt with here. Mention, however, should be made of the recent transcription of this piece into staff notation by Laurence Picken (*The New Oxford History of Music,* I, 111), in which he has repeated the mistake caused by the missing tablature. (On this problem see my the notes to the transcription.) In addition to this, there are numerous other discrepancies between Picken's version and both Yang's version and my own.

In the introduction to this composition Jiang Kwei gives very specific instructions on tuning the strings of the *chyn* for the piece: "Beginning with a *mannjyuediaw* tuning [which is C_1, D_1, E_1, G_1, A_1, C, D; see Chapter III, p. 80], first loosen the fourth string so that its first-fret note [three octaves above the fundamental] will coincide with the second string's eleventh-fret note [a major third above, that is, F_1-sharp]; then the sixth string should be loosened so that its first-fret note will coincide with the fourth string's tenth-fret note [a fourth above, that is, B_1]." (慢角調慢四一暉取二絃十一暉應慢六一暉取四絃十暉 應大絃黃鐘宮二絃黃鐘商三絃黃鐘角四絃黃鐘變徵側五絃黃鐘羽六絃 黃鐘變宮側七絃黃鐘清商.) The result is a tuning of C_1, D_1, E_1, F_1-sharp (*tseh*), A_1, B_1 (*tseh*), D. Jiang calls this tuning *tsehshangdiaw* 側商調 and defines the *tseh* types of tuning as those that contain the augmented fourth and seventh degrees (in this case, the F_1-sharp and the B_1) in the open strings. According to him, this tuning was no longer used in his time; he devised it through a study of the mode of a Tarng dynasty song, "Ijou" 伊州, which was known to be associated with the *tsehshang* tuning. The melody "Guu Yuann" was composed afterwards. (加變宮 變徵為散聲者日側弄　側商之調久亡唐人詩云側商調裏唱伊州予以此 語尋之伊州大食調黃鐘律法之商乃以慢角轉絃取變宮變徵散聲　予既 得此調因製品絃法并古怨)

There is no indication of melodic punctuation in this piece; only a comma will be used above the staff to mark phrase endings in the word text. A long wiggly line between two notes, as in the *chyn* pieces preceding, indicates a *yiin*, the portamento obtained by sliding the left-hand finger up or down along the string; the short wiggly line above a note is a *yn*, the vibrato; the small circle above a note indicates that it is in harmonics.

古怨

in harmonics

end of harmonics section

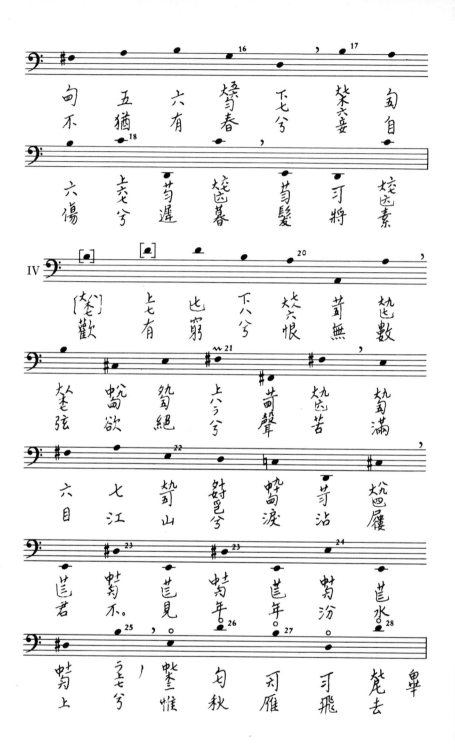

NOTES TO TRANSCRIPTION

1. The *CTTS* edition has VII_7 (d), but Yang, following the Jang edition, has VII_9 (A).

2. The *CTTS* edition has VII_9 (A); Yang has VII_7 (d).

3. Because of a similar passage in the following instrumental interlude, Yang has assigned both d and B to the character *chyan* 前 in the text and gives an extra note, A, to the character *shi* 兮. The portamento is suggested by the symbol 弓 *yiin*.

4. This is the missing note in the Luh edition which caused the shifting of the rest of the tablature to fill the gap.

5. Both the *CTTS* and the Jang editions have 芍 VI_0 (B_1) but Yang prefers to call it 芍 I_0 (C_1) here. This is one of several cases in which the character for *liow* 六 (six) is changed into *dah* 大 (big or first,) by Yang; thus the sixth string becomes the first string. Actually the two characters in the *CTTS* edition are quite distinct. Where the two readings are equally plausible stylistically, I have tried to follow the *CTTS* version, which also happens to agree with the Jang edition at these points.

6. Both the *CTTS* and the Jang editions have $IV_{8.9}$ (C-sharp), but Yang prefers to read it as $IV_{8.5}$ (D).

7. This cluster of symbols stands for *chih tour tzay tzuoh* 迄頭再作 (go back to the beginning and repeat). See page 90.

8. The Jang edition, according to Yang, has V_{10}. In harmonics it would be still an octave higher.

9. Instead of the harmonic of VI_9 (f-sharp) yang has the harmonic of VII_9 (a).

10. For the harmonic of VI_{10} (b) Yang reads the harmonic of I_{10} (c). (See note 5 above.)

11. For VI_{11} (D-sharp) Yang has I_{12} (D_1-sharp).

12. For VI_0 (B_1) Yang reads I_0 (C_1).

13. For VI_{11} (D-sharp) Yang reads $I_{10.8}$ (E_1). See Chapter III, page 79 on the adjustment for the eleventh fret.

14. In both cases, for VI_{10} (E) Yang reads I_{10} (F_1).

15. For II_{10} (G_1) Yang has $II_{\text{beyond } 13}$ (E_1). Yang's reading is preferable because it makes better sense with the following statement, 手 (move up to the tenth fret.)

16. For $II_{5.6}$ (G) Yang has $VII_{5.6}$ (g). This shows some editing beyond mere correcting of scribal errors; there is some alteration of the playing method while retaining the basic melodic line.

17. For the next three notes, VI_7, V_7, VI_7 (B, A, B) Yang's version reads VI_9, V_9, VI_9 (F-sharp, E, F-sharp). But his transcription says E, D, E (*Studies*, p. 85), which is probably a mistake even if his tablature were correct.

18. For 耄 (go up to 6.7 [on VI]: C) Yang has 奏 (go up to 6.9: B).

19. A note is missing here in all editions (see preliminary remarks to this section), making the second note (which is indicated by a fret number without a string number) also unreadable. Yang suggests 箸 VII_8, that is, B, which means the following note will be read d. The melodic motif thus formed with the succeeding three notes also appears in the two previous sections.

20. The fret position 7.8 as given in the *CTTS* edition is a little low for A. Yang suggests changing it to 7.6.

21. For 夅 V_8 (F-sharp) Yang has 夅 VI_9, which actually is also F-sharp.

22. The note 莟 $V_{2\ 9}$ (c'-sharp) followed by 慧 requires an unusually awkward jump down to the tenth fret. Since the usual approach to the latter is by a note using the ninth fret, I suggest emending this tablature to read 莟 V_9 (E). Yang has 莟 $V_{7\ 9}$ (F-sharp) and suggests the adding of an extra note E by sliding down to the ninth fret after the F.

23. See note 13 above.

24. For VI_{10} (E) Yang reads I_{10} (F).

25. Since Yang considers the previous note to be on the first string, the instruction 走 (move up to the seventh fret) would make the next note C in his transcription.

26. For the harmonic of VII_7 (d), Yang prefers to emend it and read it II_7 (D).

27. For the harmonic of VI_7 (B) Yang has the harmonic of I_7 (C).

28. In the *SBTK* edition, where the music is consistently shifted up one note, this symbol becomes aligned with the last character of the text. Picken simply supplies an extra note (d) here.

Music in the Liuhleu Notation

THE TWELVE RITUAL SONGS RECORDED BY JU SHI

1. "Luh Ming" 鹿鳴 (Iou Iou, Cry the Deer [Waley 183])
2. "Syh Moou 四牡 (My Four Steeds Are Weary [146])

3. "Hwanghwang Jee Hwa" 皇皇者華 (Bright Are the Flowers [290])
4. "Yu Lih" 魚麗 (The Fish Caught in the Trap [168])
5. "Nan Yeou Jya Yu" 南有嘉魚 (In the South There Are Lucky Fish [169])
6. "Nan Shan Yeou Tair" 南山有台 (On the Southern Hill Grows the Nutgrass [170])
7. "Guan Jiu" 關雎 (Fair, Fair, Cry the Ospreys [87])
8. "Gee Tarn" 葛覃 (How the Cloth Plant Spreads [112])
9. "Jeuan Eel" 卷耳 (Thick Grows the Cocklebur [40])
10. "Shaur Nan" 召南 (Now the Magpie Had a Nest [89])
11. "Tsae Farn" 采蘩 (See, She Gathers White Aster [98])
12. "Tsae Pyng" 采蘋 (Here We Are Gathering Duckweed [76])

PRELIMINARY REMARKS

A detailed study in English with transcriptions of these twelve pieces into staff notation has already been made by Laurence Picken ("Twelve Ritual Melodies"), who made use of most of the available editions; additional texts used here are the microfilm of the Sonq printed edition of 1217–1222 now preserved in Taiwan (see Chapter I, note 41) and the Japanese edition of 1662. I shall mention only the few discrepancies found between these additional sources and Picken's transcriptions. In the notes Picken's transcriptions are transposed down a fourth to facilitate comparison.

The various rhythmic interpretations of these songs by other transcribers have been discussed in Chapter III. I shall quote for melody Number 7 a sample of the most elaborate version, done by Chiou Jyluh in 1839 (see Yang, *History,* p. 201).

The twelve songs make use of only two modes, fa of c (Numbers 1–6) and sol of b-flat (Numbers 7–12). Ju Shi adds to the modal names the word *ching,* thus *hwang jong ching-gong* 黃鐘清宮 and *wuyih ching-shang* 無射清商, because the cadences are on the higher octave. In this respect the modal labels agree with the modes described by Sheen Gua (see above Table 3) instead of the modes in *Tsyr Yuan* or *Shyhlin Goang jih* (see Table 2).

The English titles are taken from the first lines of each poem in Arthur Waley's translation, *The Book of Songs* (London, 1937). The numbers in brackets are also Waley's. In the transcriptions a small dash across the

top line of the staff indicates the end of a phrase; the rhyme schemes of
the text, based upon Bernhard Karlgren's indications in his translation
of the *Book of Odes* (Stockholm, 1950), are indicated by small capital
letters above the staff. Where a song has more than one stanza, the
rhymes of each stanza are lettered separately.

1. 鹿鳴

呦 呦 鹿 鳴 食 野 之 苹

我 有 嘉 賓 鼓 瑟 吹 笙

吹 笙 鼓 簧 承 筐 是 將

人 之 好 我 示 我 周 行

呦 呦 鹿 鳴 食 野 之 蒿

我 有 嘉 賓 德 音 孔 昭

視 民 不 恌 君 子 是 則 是 傚

我 有 旨 酒 嘉 賓 式 燕 以 敖

呦 呦 鹿 鳴 食 野 之 苓

我 有 嘉 賓 鼓 瑟 鼓 琴

鼓 瑟 鼓 琴 和 樂 且 湛

我 有 旨 酒 以 燕 樂 嘉 賓 之 心

2. 四 牡

四 牡 騑 騑 周 道 倭 遲 豈 不

懷 歸 王 事 靡 監 我 心 傷 悲

四 牡 騑 騑 嘽 嘽 駱 馬 豈 不

懷 歸 王 事 靡 監 不 遑 啟 處

III 翩翩者鵻載飛載下集于

苞栩王事靡盬不遑將父

IV 翩翩者鵻載飛載止集于

苞杞王事靡盬不遑將母

V 駕彼四駱載驟駸駸豈不

懷歸是用作歌將母來諗

3. 皇皇者華

I 皇皇者華于彼原隰

駪駪征夫每懷靡及

4. 魚麗

5. 南有嘉魚

I

南　有　嘉　魚　烝　然　罩　罩

君　子　有　酒　嘉　賓　式　燕　以　樂

II

南　有　嘉　魚　烝　然　汕　汕

君　子　有　酒　嘉　賓　式　燕　以　衎

III

南　有　樛　木　甘　瓠　纍　之

君　子　有　酒　嘉　賓　式　燕　綏　之

IV

翩　翩　者　鵻　烝　然　來　思

君　子　有　酒　嘉　賓　式　燕　又　思

[162]

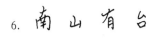

6. 南山有台

南 山 有 台 北 山 有 萊

樂 只 君 子 邦 家 之 基

樂 只 君 子 萬 壽 無 期

南 山 有 桑 北 山 有 楊

樂 只 君 子 邦 家 之 光

樂 只 君 子 萬 壽 無 疆

7. 關雎

關 關 雎 鳩 在 河 之 洲

窈 窕 淑 女 君 子 好 逑

參 差 荇 菜 左 右 流 之

窈 窕 淑 女 寤 寐 求 之

求 之 不 得 寤 寐 思 服

悠 哉 悠 哉 輾 轉 反 側

參 差 荇 菜 左 右 采 之

窈 窕 淑 女 琴 瑟 友 之

参 差 荇 菜 左 右 芼 之

窈 窕 淑 女 鍾 鼓 樂 之

Chiou Jyluh's interpretation of the same piece

[sic]

8. 葛覃

9. 卷耳

采采卷耳 不盈頃筐

嗟我懷人 寘彼周行

陟彼崔嵬 我馬虺隤

我姑酌彼金罍 維以不永懷

陟彼高岡 我馬玄黃 我姑

酌彼兕觥 維以不永傷

陟彼砠矣 我馬瘏矣

我僕痛矣 云何吁矣

10. 召南

I 維 鵲 有 巢 維 鳩 居 之

之 子 于 歸 百 兩 御 之

II 維 鵲 有 巢 維 鳩 方 之

之 子 于 歸 百 兩 將 之

III 維 鵲 有 巢 維 鳩 盈 之

之 子 于 歸 百 兩 成 之

11. 采蘩

于 以 采 蘩 于 沼 于 沚

于 以 用 之 公 侯 之 事

于 以 采 蘩 于 澗 之 中

于 以 用 之 公 侯 之 宮

被 之 僮 僮 夙 夜 在 公

被 之 祁 祁 薄 言 還 歸

12. 采蘋

于 以 采 蘋 南 澗 之 濱

于 以 采 藻 于 彼 行 潦

于 以 盛 之 維 筐 及 筥

于 以 湘 之 維 錡 及 釜

于 以 奠 之 宗 室 牖 下

誰 其 尸 之 有 齊 季 女

TRANSCRIPTIONS

1. The 1662 edition has c′, a here.
2. The 1662 edition has a in these two places.
3. Picken has d′.
4. The 1662 edition has c′.
5. Picken has c here.
6. The 1662 and the Sonq edition (which is emended at this point) have a here.
7. The 1662 and the Sonq editions have e, but the microfilm of the latter reveals that the woodcut has been corrected from the character *tay* 太 (d). Picken has d here.

THE TEN RITUAL SONGS FOR *YUEH* BY JIANG KWEI

I. "Dih Shuenn Chuu Diaw" 帝舜楚調 (Emperor Shuenn)
II. "Wang Yeu Wu Diaw" 王禹吳調 (King Yu)
III. "Yueh Wang Yueh Diaw" 越王越調 (The King of Yueh)
IV. "Yueh Shianq Tsehshangdiaw" 越相側商調 (The Minister of Yueh)
V. "Shianq Wang Guu Pyngdiaw" 項王古平調 (The King of Shianq)
VI. "Taur Jy Shern Shuangdiaw" 濤之神雙調 (The Spirit of the Waves)
VII. "Tsaur Er Shuu Tsehdiaw" 曹娥蜀側調 (The Filial Daughter Tsaur Er)
VIII. "Parng Jiangjiun Gau Pyngdiaw" 龐將軍高平調 (General Parng)
IX. "Jing Jong Jonggoan Shangdiaw" 旌忠中管商調 (The Loyal Subjects)
X. "Tsay Shiaw Tzyy Jonggoan Banjandiaw" 蔡孝子中管般瞻調 (The Filial Son of Tsay)

As with the other compositions in Jiang Kwei's collection, the transcription of these songs is based on the *CTTS* edition collated with the *SBTK* edition. A detailed comparison was also made with the transcription by Yang Yinnliou, who used essentially the Jang edition. (See remarks on editions preceding the transcriptions of Jiang Kwei's Seventeen *Tsyr* Songs in the popular notation.) A detailed study of both the text and the music of these songs has also been done by Laurence Picken ("Nine Songs"). Although he used the same editions as those used for the present transcriptions, there are a few differences in the results, and in two instances he even punctuates the text differently. Both Yang's and Picken's readings are discussed in the notes. As a sample of Yang's rhythmic application his version of the first piece, *Studies,* page 88, is given (see Chapter III, note 10). It has been transposed to the key used in the present transcription.

With the exception of Numbers 1 and 6 Jiang has given the classical modal name of each piece. In addition he supplies for each another modal name, of which some are the correct counterparts in the popular nomenclature (Numbers 3, 6, 8, and 9), and others are of obscure origin, such as *Guu pyngdiaw* 古平調 (Number 5) and *Shuu tsehdiaw* 蜀側調 (Number 7). *Tsehshangdiaw* 側商調 (Number 4) is discussed above, in the introduction to Jiang Kwei's song with *chyn* accompaniment, "Guu Yuann." The names *Chuu diaw* 楚調 (Number 1) and *Wu diaw* 吳調 (Number 2) and *Yueh diaw* 吳調 (Number 3) are obviously allusions to the three ancient southern states of Chuu, Wu, and Yueh; the last of this group also happens to be the real popular name for the mode.

It has been noted before that some of the songs in this group have melodic materials in common with some of Jiang Kwei's *tsyr* songs. Since this group is written in the completely fixed-pitch *liuhleu* notation, while the *tsyr* songs are in the variable popular notation, it might be thought that the *liuhleu* notation could have helped to decide the reading of some of the questionable notes in the *tsyr* songs, in particular, the choice between d′ and e′-flat for the symbol *wuu* (see Chapter III, page 60). However, for some unknown reason, Jiang used only one reading, d′, throughout the songs in this group where the two possibilities theoretically exist.

For translation of the text of these songs, see Picken, *Studies.*

The rhyme schemes of these Ritual Songs are difficult to establish. Jiang Kwei could have used (1) the so-called *pyngshoei* system of 106 rhymes of the late Sonq period (see Wang Lih, *Hannyeu Inyunn* [Chinese Phonology] Peking, 1963, p. 63); (2) the Tarng dynasty system of 206 rhymes; or (3) some kind of pre-Chyn or archaic rhyming system (since Jiang Kwei was supposed to have modeled his Ritual Songs after the *Chuu Tsyr*). I have made a comparison of the three types of rhyme by applying each to the phrase endings of the Ritual Songs and found that the *pyngshoei* reading gives by far the greatest number of rhyming phrases. (The second and third schemes are based upon Bernhard Karlgren's reconstruction of ancient and archaic Chinese pronunciation in his *Grammata Serica Recensa*, Stockholm, 1957, and the first is based upon the *pyngshoei* rhymes given in Herbert A. Giles's *A Chinese-English Dictionary*, Shanghai, 1892.) Therefore I have adopted essentially this system in marking the rhyming words for the present transcription. Laurence Picken, on the other hand, chose the Tarng system, based on Karlgren's *Analytic Dictionary of Chinese and Sino-Japanese* (Paris, 1923). It must be borne in mind that there are also places where the archaic reading seems preferable, for example, 1.II, 2.I, 4.I, 10.I. There is at least one place, 7.IV, where the Tarng reading is preferable; and in many cases, 1.III, 4.II, 5.I, II, III, 8.II, 8.V, all three seem equally good. In some places a word must have been a rhyme word by virtue of its position and close assonance, even though none of the three systems mentioned above qualifies it. Since this is not a historical linguistic study but simply an attempt to show where the rhyme words are located in the music I have made emendations in marking the rhyme scheme in the following pieces: 1.I, 2.III, 5.II, 6.I, 8.III.

1. 帝舜楚調

央 央 帝 旂 群 晁 相 興

聿 來 我 嫣 我 芸 綠 滋

維 相 與 楚 謂 狩 在 陼

雲 橫 九 疑 帝 若 來 下

我 懷 厭 初 熟 耕 熟 漁

忽 忘 惠 康 疇 匪 帝 餘

博 碩 于 俎 維 錯 于 豆

瑤 灑 玉 離 侑 此 桂 酒

Yang Yinnliou's interpretation of the same piece

3. 越王越調

sol of b-flat

I 雲 蒼 涼 山 截 岸 A

瞻 靈 旗 闖 越 絕

故 宮 淒 淒 生 綠 蕪 A

II 謀 臣 安 在 空 五 湖

醉 君 君 毋 西 入 吳 A

III 洪 濤 卷 地 龍 工 呼 A

函 堅 操 刓 何 雕 肝 A

彼 茁 竹 箭 楊 梅 朱

[179]

4. 越相側商調

壺觴有酌盤有魚

千春萬春勿忘此故都

淒其我思永矢弗遊

鳥日予肖以璺與鏐

載尸載謁子惠思越

翩其來而乘濤駕月

5. 項王古平調

fa of b-flat

I 民 茶 蠃 天 紀 瀆

羣 雄 橫 徂 君 逐 鹿

傳 懸 於 投 匪 智 伊 福

II 或 肉 以 昌 或 斧 以 亡

謂 予 復 歸 有 如 大 江

III 我 無 君 尤 君 胡 我 慊

亦 有 子 孫 在 阿 在 崦

IV 靈 兮 歸 來 築 宮 崔 嵬

[181]

6. 濤之神雙調

7. 曹娥蜀側調

玉 副 箏 錦 結 襦 含 清

揚 兮 鬱 翠 眉 嚶 嚶 歌 兮

有 待 柳 屢 舞 兮 傲 傲

昔 何 止 兮 水 湄 今 何

徵 兮 未 來 吾 無 欲 兮 女

之 佩 羌 猶 豫 兮 而 裴 回

黃 頭 兮 呼 風 旗 尾 兮 栩 栩

潮 枯 兮 沙 遲 將 子 兮 無 怒

舟 去 兮 無 歸 花 落 兮 鳥 啼

8. 龐將軍高平調

鞭 臥 龍 躍 鏡 浦 靈 之 來 瞳 如 雨

環 玉 廂 翠 繽 紛 靈 之 逝 扉 出 雲

我 行 其 野 有 稌 有 稌

入 其 闤 闍 載 歌 載 舞

祓 我 家 室 曰 予 父 母

高 田 萊 蕪 下 田 烏 卤

爾 澤 毋 三 爾 煦

毋 五 益 嚴 祀 其 終 古

9. 旌忠中管商調

師 環 城 兮 鳥 不 度

萬 夫 投 戈 兮 子 獨 武

車 轍 屬 兮 螳 螂 怒

抗 予 義 兮 出 行 伍

詩 書 發 冢 兮 嗟 彼 傖 父

父 老 死 兮 後 生 莫 知 其 故

廟 無 人 兮 鼠 穴 堵

歌 予 詩 兮 詔 萬 古

10. 蔡孝子中管般瞻調

re of d-flat [14]

I

愛予親兮保予體將臨淵

A [16] [15] A

兮髮上指予青衿兮父為史

[15] A

不如縗絰兮鬱陶以死

A

II

豹為政兮吾已矣望大淵

[15]

淪兮倏而逝臥龍山兮

A A

若耶水靈不歸兮父思子

[15]

III

雨鳴荷兮風入葦

A

若伊優兮泣未已犖我

[17] A

子兮與弟屋陽阿兮招爾

NOTES TO TRANSCRIPTIONS

1. Yang has f.

2. Yang has c′.

3. Yang gives this and the following two notes an octave lower.

4. Yang has a, g instead of g, a.

5. The *CTTS* edition has the character *dah* 大 (d-flat), which should be *tay* 太 (d).

6. Picken has e-flat.

7. Picken considers this character the last word of the previous phrase, whereas Yang cuts the phrase just before this word (which also agrees with the punctuated *TSJC* edition of Jiang Kwei's songs). According to Picken (*Nine Songs,* p. 212) the text reads:

嚶嚶歌兮有待柳

屢舞兮傲傲

which he translates, "With song as of a bird calling its fellows she is a waiting willow, Ofttimes she dances, dances drunkenly." If we give the character *leou* 柳 to the next phrase the meaning would be: "With song as of a bird calling and waiting for its fellows, her willowy figure constantly dances drunkenly." In this second version the music agrees with the phrasing in the next stanza.

8. Picken has c′.

9. The small cross, meaning "slightly higher than the written note," is used here for the term *jertzyh* 折字 (see page 70). The following is Yang's interpretation of the same passage in which he adds the short extra note g for *jertzyh.*

10. Yang uses an extra note for *jertzyh.*

11. Yang gives this a simple c′.

12. The *CTTS* edition has *lin* 林 (g), which does not belong to the mode. Yang's choice is a.

13. These are the places where *tay* 太 (d') instead of *dah* 大 (d'flat) appears in all editions. Yang and Picken have also made emendations here.

14. The special modal name for this piece 中管般瞻調 must be an alternate form of 高般涉調 which is the regular popular name for re of d-flat.

15. See note 13.

16. Picken has c.

17. Both Picken and Yang have a-flat. Picken considers this word of the text to be the last character of the previous phrase, whereas the *TSJC* version and Yang's reading punctuate the phrase just before this character.

THE THIRTY-ONE CEREMONIAL SONGS BY SHYONG| PER'NGLAI|

1. "Tzou Yu" 騶虞 (Strong Grow the Reeds [Waley 207])
2. "Tzou Yu" 騶虞 (Strong Grow the Reeds)
3. "Chyi Yuh" 淇澳 (Look at the Little Bay of Chyi [42])
4. "Kao Parn" 考槃 (Drumming and Dancing in the Gulley [15])
5. "Shuu Li" 黍離 (That Wine Millet Bends under Its Weight [273])
6. "Tzy I" 緇衣 (How Well Your Black Coat Fits [11])
7. "Far Tarn" 伐檀 (Chop, Chop They Cut the Hard Woods [259])
8. "Jian Jea" 蒹葭 (Thick Grow the Rush Leaves [34])
9. "Herng Men" 衡門 (Down Blow the Town Gate [13])
10. "Chi Yueh" 七月 (In the Seventh Month the Fire Ebbs [159])
11. "Jingjing Jee Er" 菁菁者莪 (Thick Grows the Tarragon [111])
12. "Heh Ming" 鶴鳴 (When the Crane Cries at the Nine Swamps [281])
13. "Bor Jiu" 白駒 (Unsullied the White Colt [185])
14. "Wen Wang" 文王 (When King Wen is on High [241])
15. "Yih: Bor Guei" 抑:白圭 (Grave and Dignified Manners: Section Five [271])
16. "Yih: Shianq Tzay Eel 抑:相在爾 (Grave and Dignified Manners: Section Seven)
17. "Sonq Gau" 崧高 (Mightiest of All Heights in the Peak [137])
18. "Jeng Min" 烝民 (The People of Our Race Were Created by Heaven [142])

19. "Ching Miaw" 清廟 (Solemn the Hallowed Temple [214])
20. "Tzay Shan" 載芟(They Clear Away the Grass, the Trees [157])
21. "Liang Syh" 良耜 (Very Sharp, the Good Shares [158])
22. "Jiong" 駉 (Stout and Strong, Our Stallions [252])
23. "Yng Shern Ning'an Jy Cheu" 迎神凝安之曲 (Welcoming the Gods)
24. "Guannshii Torng'an Jy Cheu" 盥洗同安之曲 (The Purification)
25. "Tzuen Bih Ming'an Jy Cheu" 尊幣明安之曲 (Offering of Gifts)
26. "Jwoshiann Cherng'an Jy Cheu: Shian Shenq" 酌獻成安之曲：先聖 (Offering of Entertainment to the Former Sages)
27. "Yeangwo Gong Yann Tzyy" 兗國公顏子 (Honoring Yan Tzyy)
28. "Chernggwo Gong Tzeng Tzyy" 成國公曾子 (Honoring Tzeng Tzyy)
29. "Yigwo Gong Tzyy Sy" 沂國宮子思 (Honoring Tzyy Sy)
30. "Tzougwo Gong Menq Tzyy" 鄒國公孟子 (Honoring Menq Tzyy)
31. "Sonq Shern Ning'an Jy Cheu" 送神寧安之曲 (Sending Off the Gods)

PRELIMINARY REMARKS

Two editions are used for these transcriptions: the *TSJC* edition (which is a photolithographic reproduction of the *Jyy Hae* edition of 1846), and the *Jing Yuan* edition of 1847.

A special word must be said about the names of the modes used by Shyong. For each piece he gives both the classical and the popular modal names; in most cases the pairing of the two kinds of names agree with other Sonq sources, such as *Shyhlin Goangjih* and *Tsyr Yuan*. The majority of the modal names seem to fit the music, but the melodies in the la modes all seem to have the final notes a fifth too low. As noted before, in actual practice during Sonq the la modes were transposed a fifth higher than the original pitches and adopted the popular name of the other modes at this pitch. While using the popular names currently in fashion, Shyong must have composed the la-mode melodies in the original key.

In his introduction (1. 12) Shyong mentions that the zither accompaniment should be played with two hands an octave apart. Yang Yinnliou has transcribed melody Number 7 according to this description and given it a rhythmic interpretation in 2/4 meter (see Chapter III, note 126; Yang, *Illustrations,* p. 14). The voice part of Yang's transcription will be quoted here.

Shyong does not use the prefix *ching* to indicate octave notes. But as every piece is presented also in the *gongcheh* notation which does distinguish the different octaves, the correct pitch is clear. Many examples show that Shyong did not follow very closely the current practice in the use of modes: in the thirty-one pieces he used no less than twenty different modes; sixteen pieces are in nine modes which are not in current use. In nine pieces where choices were to be made between d' and e'-flat Shyong uses both notes. In two pieces belonging to the sol of g mode which are on pentatonic scales (see above, Table 3) Shyong has used the augmented fourth degree, c-sharp.

The English titles of Numbers 1–22 are from the first lines of Waley's translation in *The Book of Songs;* the numbers indicated in brackets are also Waley's.

For Numbers 1–12 the rhyme schemes of the texts are based upon Karlgren's *Book of Odes.* Numbers 22–31 are songs written by Shyong Pernglai himself; he could have used one of the three possible types of rhyming systems known in his time (see preliminary remarks to Jiang Kwei's Ritual Songs). After spot checking a few lines, it became clear that the late Sonq system of 106 *pyngshoei* rhymes is preferable. I have again made some emendations in marking the rhyme schemes in the following pieces: 23.I, III, 24, 27, and 29. It is to be noted that some songs are really only different settings of the same text.

1. 騶虞

彼 茁 者 葭 壹 發

五 豝 于 嗟 乎 騶 虞

彼 茁 者 蓬 壹 發

五 豵 于 嗟 乎 騶 虞

2. 騶虞

彼 茁 者 葭 壹 發

五 豝 于 嗟 乎 騶 虞

彼 茁 者 蓬 壹 發

五 豵 于 嗟 乎 騶 虞

3. 淇澳

sol of b-flat

瞻 彼 淇 澳 綠 竹 猗 猗

有 匪 君 子 如 切 如 磋 如 琢

如 磨 瑟 兮 僩 兮 赫 兮 喧 兮

有 匪 君 子 終 不 可 諼 兮

瞻 彼 淇 澳 綠 竹 青 青

有 匪 君 子 充 耳 琇 瑩 會 弁

如 星 瑟 兮 僩 兮 赫 兮 喧 兮

有 匪 君 子 終 不 可 諼 兮

4. 考槃

5. 黍離

彼 黍 離 離 彼 稷 之 穗

行 邁 靡 靡 中 心 如 醉 知 我 者

謂 我 心 憂 不 知 我 者 謂 我

何 求 悠 悠 蒼 天 此 何 人 哉

彼 黍 離 離 彼 稷 之 實

行 邁 靡 靡 中 心 如 噎 知 我 者

謂 我 心 憂 不 知 我 者 謂 我

何 求 悠 悠 蒼 天 此 何 人 哉

6. 緇衣

7. 伐檀

不稼不穡　胡取禾三百億兮

不狩不獵　胡瞻爾庭有縣

特兮彼君子兮不素食兮

坎坎伐輪兮寘之河

之漘兮河水清且淪猗

不稼不穡　胡取禾三百囷兮

不狩不獵　胡瞻爾庭有縣

鶉兮彼君子兮不素飧兮

Yang Inliou's version of the first stanza (voice only)

8. 蒹葭

蒹葭蒼蒼 白露為霜
所謂伊人 在水一方
遡洄從之 道阻且長
遡游從之 宛在水中央

[199]

蒹 葭 淒 淒 白 露 未 晞

所 謂 伊 人 在 水 之 湄

溯 洄 從 之 道 阻 且 躋

遡 游 從 之 宛 在 水 中 坻

蒹 葭 采 采 白 露 未 已

所 謂 伊 人 在 水 之 涘

遡 洄 從 之 道 阻 且 右

遡 游 從 之 宛 在 水 中 沚

9. 衡門

衡 門 之 下 可 以 棲 遲

泌 之 洋 洋 可 以 樂 飢

豈 其 食 魚 必 河 之 魴

豈 其 取 妻 必 齊 之 姜

豈 其 食 魚 必 河 之 鯉

豈 其 取 妻 必 宋 之 子

10. 七 月

春 日 遲 遲 采 繁 祁 祁

女 心 傷 悲 殆 及 公 子 同 歸

la of e ³

七 月 流 火 八 月 萑 葦

蠶 月 條 桑 取 彼 斧 斨

以 伐 遠 揚 猗 彼 女 桑 七 月

鳴 鵙 八 月 載 績 載 玄 載 黃

我 朱 孔 陽 為 公 子 裳

la of d-flat

四 月 秀 葽 五 月 鳴 蜩

八 月 其 穫 十 月 隕 蘀 一 之

日 于 貉 取 彼 狐 貍 為 公 子 裘

二 之 日 其 同 載 纘 武 功

言 私 其 豵 獻 豣 于 公

五 月 斯 螽 動 股 六 月

莎 雞 振 羽 七 月 在 野 八 月

在 宇 九 月 在 戶 十 月 蟋 蟀

入 我 牀 下 穹 窒 熏 鼠 塞 向 墐 戶

嗟 我 婦 子 曰 為 改 歲 入 此 室 處

sol of b-flat

VI

六 月 食 鬱 及 薁 七 月

烹 葵 及 菽 八 月 剝 棗 十 月

穫 稻 為 此 春 酒 以 介 眉 壽

七 月 食 瓜 八 月 斷 壺 九 月

叔 苴 采 荼 薪 樗 食 我 農 夫

la of d

VII

九 月 築 場 圃 十 月 納

禾 稼 黍 稷 重 穋 禾 麻 菽 麥

嗟 我 農 夫 我 稼 既 同

上 入 執 宮 功 畫 爾 于 茅 宵 爾

索 綯 亟 其 乘 屋 其 始 播 百 穀

二 之 日 鑿 冰 沖 沖

三 之 日 納 于 凌 陰 四 之 日

其 蚤 獻 羔 祭 韭 九 月 肅 霜

十 月 滌 場 朋 酒 斯 饗

日 殺 羔 羊 躋 彼 公 堂

稱 彼 兕 觥 萬 壽 無 疆

11. 菁菁者莪

fa of e-flat

I

菁 菁 者 莪 在 彼 中 阿

既 見 君 子 樂 且 有 儀

II

菁 菁 者 莪 在 彼 中 沚

既 見 君 子 我 心 則 喜

III

菁 菁 者 莪 在 彼 中 陵

既 見 君 子 錫 我 百 朋

IV

汎 汎 楊 舟 載 沉 載 浮

既 見 君 子 我 心 則 休

12. 鶴鳴

fa of c

I

鶴 鳴 于 九 皐 聲 聞 于 野

魚 潛 在 淵 或 在 于 渚 樂 彼

之 園 爰 有 樹 檀 其 下 維 蘀

他 山 之 石 可 以 為 錯

II

鶴 鳴 于 九 皐 聲 聞 于 天

魚 在 于 渚 或 潛 在 淵 樂 彼

之 園 爰 有 樹 檀 其 下 維 穀

他 山 之 石 可 以 攻 玉

13. 白駒

皎皎白駒 食我場苗

縶之維之 以永今朝

所謂伊人 於焉逍遥

皎皎白駒 食我場藿

縶之維之 以永今夕

所謂伊人 於焉嘉客

皎皎白駒 賁然來思

爾公爾侯 逸豫無期

14. 文王

fa of d-flat

VI

無 念 爾 祖 聿 修 厥 德

永 言 配 命 自 求 多 福

殷 之 未 喪 師 克 配 上 帝

宜 鑒 于 殷 駿 命 不 易

fa of c

VII

命 之 不 易 無 遏 爾 躬

宣 昭 義 問 有 虞 殷 自 天

上 天 之 載 無 聲 無 臭

儀 刑 文 王 萬 邦 作 孚

[213]

15. 抑：白圭

sol of f

質爾人民　謹爾侯度

用戒不虞　慎爾出話

敬爾威儀　無不柔嘉

白圭之玷　尚可磨也

斯言之玷　不可為也

16. 抑：相在爾

sol of c

視爾友君子　輯柔爾顏

不遐有愆　相在爾室

尚 不 愧 于 屋 漏 無 日 不 顯

莫 予 云 覯 神 之 格 思

不 可 度 思 矧 可 射 思

17. 崧 高

sol of g

崧 高 維 嶽 駿 極 于 天

維 嶽 降 神 生 甫 及 申

維 申 及 甫 維 周 之 翰

四 國 于 蕃 四 方 于 宣

18. 烝民

sol of c

天 生 烝 民 有 物 有 則

民 之 秉 彝 好 是 懿 德

天 監 有 周 昭 假 于 下

保 茲 天 子 生 仲 山 甫

19. 清廟

fa of e-flat

於 穆 清 廟 肅 雝 顯 相

濟 濟 多 士 秉 文 之 德

對 越 在 天 駿 奔 走 在 廟

不 顯 不 承 無 射 於 人 斯

20. 載芟

fa of e-flat

載芟載柞 其耕澤澤

千耦其耘 徂隰徂畛

侯主侯伯 侯亞侯旅

侯彊侯以 有嗿其饁

思媚其婦 有依其士

有略其耜 俶載南畝

播厥百穀 實函斯活

驛驛其達　有厭其傑

厭厭其苗　緜緜其麃

載獲濟濟　有實其積

萬億及秭　為酒為醴

烝畀祖妣　以洽百禮

有飶其香　邦家之光

有椒其馨　胡考之寧　匪且

有且匪今　斯今振古如茲

21. 良耜

畟 畟 良 耜 俶 載 南 畝

播 厥 百 穀 實 函 斯 活

或 來 瞻 女 載 筐 及 筥

其 饟 伊 黍 其 笠 伊 糾

其 鎛 斯 趙 以 薅 荼 蓼

荼 蓼 朽 止 黍 稷 茂 止

穫 之 挃 挃 積 之 栗 栗

其 崇 如 墉 其 比 如 櫛

以 開 百 室 百 室 盈 止

婦 子 寧 止 殺 時 犉 牡 有 捄

有 角 以 似 以 續 續 古 之 人

22. 駉

sol of g

駉 駉 牡 馬 在 坰 之 野

薄 言 駉 者 有 驈 有 皇

有 驪 有 黃 以 車 彭 彭

思 無 邪 思 馬 斯 徂

23. 迎神凝安之曲

fa of c ^{8}

I

大 哉 宜 聖 道 尊 德 崇

維 持 王 化 斯 文 是 宗

典 祀 有 常 精 純 並 隆

神 其 來 格 於 昭 盛 容

la of d-flat

II

仰 之 彌 高 式 瞻 在 前

於 昭 斯 文 被 于 萬 年

有 嚴 學 宮 神 其 來 止

思 報 無 窮 敢 忘 子 始

道 同 于 天 人 倫 之 至

有 饗 無 窮 其 興 萬 世

旣 潔 斯 牲 粢 明 醑 旨

不 解 以 忱 神 其 來 暨

生 而 知 之 有 教 無 私

永 言 其 道 萬 世 之 師

良 日 維 丁 靈 承 不 爽

揭 此 精 虔 神 其 來 饗

24. 盥洗同安之曲

fa of e

右 文 興 化 憲 古 師 經

明 祖 有 典 吉 日 維 丁

盥 洗 在 阼 雅 奏 在 庭

周 旋 登 降 福 祉 是 膺

25. 尊幣明安之曲

fa of e-flat

維 仲 之 春 興 其 秩 節

旨 酒 斯 陳 明 粢 旣 潔

洋　洋　如　臨　三　千　在　列

用　幣　將　誠　精　忱　洞　徹

晨　幾　飛　霜　聲　初　諧　商

事　先　陳　幣　恭　宜　承　筐

由　階　載　升　于　位　肅　將

周　旋　無　譁　如　在　洋　洋

26. 酌獻成安之曲洗聖

fa of e-flat

I

惟 天 何 言 惟 聖 同 天

自 有 生 民 盛 莫 加 焉

清 酤 旣 載 歌 諧 樂 聲

聿 興 斯 文 允 矣 大 成

fa of a

II

惟 天 何 言 惟 聖 同 天

自 有 生 民 盛 莫 加 焉

清 酤 旣 載 歌 諧 樂 聲

聿 興 斯 文 允 矣 大 成

27. 兗國公顏子

fa of e-flat

I 庶 幾 屢 空 簞 瓢 內 樂

聖 師 日 賢 獨 稱 好 學

與 饗 在 堂 情 文 實 稱

萬 年 承 休 假 哉 天 命

fa of a

II 庶 幾 屢 空 簞 瓢 內 樂

聖 師 日 賢 獨 稱 好 學

與 饗 在 堂 情 文 實 稱

萬 年 承 休 假 哉 天 命

28. 成國公曾子

I — fa of e-flat

心 傳 忠 恕 一 以 貫 之

爰 述 大 學 萬 世 訓 彝

惠 我 光 明 尊 聞 行 知

繼 聖 迪 後 是 饗 是 宜

II — fa of a

心 傳 忠 恕 一 以 貫 之

爰 述 大 學 萬 世 訓 彝

惠 我 光 明 尊 聞 行 知

繼 聖 迪 後 是 饗 是 宜

[227]

29. 沂國公子思

30. 鄒國公孟子

fa of e-flat

I 斷 斷 周 道 狂 瀾 倒 溁

躬 承 辟 闢 高 配 禹 功

世 隆 興 文 盛 典 惟 修

今 樂 猶 古 式 薦 春 秋

fa of a

II 斷 斷 周 道 狂 瀾 倒 溁

躬 承 辟 闢 高 配 禹 功

[229]

世 隆 興 文 盛 典 惟 修

今 樂 猶 古 式 薦 春 秋

31. 送神寧安之曲

肅 莊 神 纓 吉 蠲 牲 犧

於 皇 明 祀 登 薦 惟 時

神 之 來 兮 肸 蠁 之 隨

神 之 去 兮 休 嘉 之 貽

TRANSCRIPTIONS

1. The popular name here should properly be *shuang jyue* 雙角 instead of *shuangdiaw* 雙調 given by Shyong.

2. Shyong calls this mode (sol of a), the *shii-in* 喜音 (cheerful mode). The mode of the following piece he calls the *bei-in* 悲音 (sad mode). The pair is chosen deliberately for contrast.

3. In the *TSJC* edition this mode is called *gushean-shang* 姑洗商 (sol of e). But according to the music it should be *gushean-jyue* 姑洗角 (la of e). The *Jing Yuan* edition has 以姑洗商為角, which does not make sense.

4. In the *gongcheh* notation the *TSJC* edition says *farn* 凡, which would be b-flat. The *Jing Yuan* edition has *cheh* 尺 (g), which agrees with the *liuhleu* notation in both editions.

5. This and the next four notes are c′, g, f, g, b-flat in the *Jing Yuan* edition.

6. Shyong's label says *yinq jong-yeu* 應鐘羽 (mi of b), but the music shows that it should be called *yinq jong-jyue* 應鐘角 (la of b). This is further confirmed by the popular name *jonggoan-yueh jyuediaw* 中管越角調.

7. Shyong has *jongleu-gong* 中呂宮 (fa of f), but it should be *jongleu-shang* 中呂商 (sol of f).

8. The use of the four modes for the sections in this piece is inspired by a passage from the Classic *Jou Lii* 周禮, "Dah Sy Yueh" 大司樂 (Section on Music), which says: *hwang jong* wei *gong*, *dahleu* wei *jyue*, *taytsow* wei *jyy*, *yinq jong* wei *yeu* 黃鐘為宮, 大呂為角, 太簇為徵, 應鐘為羽 (literally, fa being on c, la being on d-flat, do being on d, mi being on b). However, the melodies show that Shyong read them: *hwang jong* jy *gong*, *dahleu* jy *jyue*, and so forth (fa of c, la of d-flat, do of d, and mi of b). On the confusion of the terms *jy* 之 and *wei* 為 in the Sonq modes, see above, pages 55–56.

9. The *liuhleu* notation has *yi* 夷 (a-flat), but the *gongcheh* notation has *i* 一 (e-flat). According to the mode of the piece, the latter is correct.

Selected Bibliography

Index

Selected Bibliography

Translations of titles that are adopted from other sources are given in parentheses rather than brackets.

PRIMARY SOURCES

1. Abe Suenao 安倍季尚 (1622–1708), *Gakkaroku* 樂家録 [A Musician's Notes]. Fifty chapters. In *Nihon Koten Zenshu* [Complete Japanese Classics], vols. XIX–XXIII.

2. Chern Yang 陳暘, *Yueh Shu* 樂書 [Treatise on Music]. Two hundred chapters. Preface dated 1104. References are to the collated edition of 1876.

3. Chern Yuanjinq 陳元靚 (ca. 1270), *Shyhlin Goangjih* 事林廣記 [A Broad Record of the Forest of Affairs]. Unless otherwise specified, page references are to the Japanese edition published in 1684 by the Rakuyō Book Store (洛陽書肆) and reprinted in 1699.

4. Cherng Shyong 程雄, *Songfengger Chyn Puu* 松風閣琴譜 [*Chyn* Music from the Pine-Wind Studio]. Two volumes, 1677.

5. *Chindinq Tsyr Puu* 欽定詞譜 (The Imperial Register of *Tz'u* Prosody), compiled by Wang Yihching 王奕清, et al., 1715. Forty chapters.

6. Chiou Jyluh 邱之稑, *Liuhin Hueykao* 律音彙考 [Studies on the (Confucian Ceremonial) Music], 1835 and 1897.

7. Duann Anjye 段安節 (late ninth century), *Yuehfuu Tzarluh* 樂府雜録 [Miscellaneous Notes on Songs]. One chapter. *Tsorngshu Jyicherng* edition.

8. *Guuchyn Cheu Hueybian* 古琴曲彙編 [A Repertory of *Chyn* Music] Transcription of actual *Chyn* performances by Shiah Ifeng, 夏一峯, and others, Ed. by Yang Yinnliou. Seventeen pieces, The Institute of Ethnomusicology 民族音樂研究所 Series. Peking, 1957, 96 pp.

9. *Guuchyn Cheu Jyi* 古琴曲集 [A Collection of *Chyn* Music]. Compiled by the Institute for the Study of Chinese Music (中國音樂研究所). Transcription of forty-one pieces (or sixty-two including variations) as performed by twenty-four different *chyn* players. Peking, 1962, 280 pp.

10. Jang Heh 張鶴, *Chyn Shyue Ruhmen* 琴學入門 [Introduction to the Study of the *Chyn*]. Two volumes. Shanghai, 1864.

11. Jang Yan 張炎 (1248–ca. 1315), *Tsyr Yuan* 詞源 [Sources of the *Tsyr*]. In two sections. Punctuated and annotated by Tsay Jen 蔡楨 in *Jin Dah Jonggwo Wenhuah Yanjiousuoo Tsorngkan* 金大中國文化研究所叢刊 [Publications of the Cultural Institute of Jinling University], Nanking, 1932, under the title of *Tsyr Yuan Shujenq*.

12. Jiang Kwei 姜夔, *Bairshyr Dawren Gecheu* 白石道人歌曲 [The Songs of Whitestone the Taoist]. Six chapters, 1202. In *Chyangtsuen Tsorngshu* 彊村叢書, vol. XVIII.

13. Jou Derching 周德清, *Jongyuan Inyunn Jenqyeu Tzuohtsyr Chiilih* 中原音韻 正語作詞起例 [Rules for Diction and Composing *Tsyr* in Chinese]. Two chapters, 1324. Yuan edition photolithographed in 1922.

14. Jou Mih 周密 (1232–1308), *Chyidong Yeeyeu* 齊東野語 [Words of a Fool from Chyidong]. Twenty chapters. *Shyuejing Taoyuan* 學津討源 edition.

15. ——— *Wuulin Jiowshyh* 武林舊事 [Memoirs from Wuulin]. Ten chapters, completed 1280–1290. References are to the edition by the Classics Press (古典文學出版社), Shanghai, 1956.

16. Ju Charngwen 朱長文 (1041–1100), *Chyn Shyy* 琴史 [History of the *Chyn*]. Preface dated 1084. Six chapters, in *Lianntyng Shyrell Joong* 楝亭十二種, Yangchow, 1921.

17. Ju Chyuan 朱權 (early fifteenth century), *Tayher Jenqin Puu* 太和正音譜 [A Song-composing Handbook of the Era of Universal Harmony]. Harnfen Lou 涵芬樓 edition.

18. Ju Shi 朱熹 (1130–1200), "Chyn Liuh Shuo" 琴律説 [Discourses on the Pitches of the *Chyn*] in *Ju Tzyy Dahchyuan* 朱子大全 (also known as *Hueyan Jyi* 晦庵集 and 晦庵先生朱文公文集). Edition, chap. 66, pp. 30a–39b.

19. ——— *Ju Tzyy Yeu Ley* 朱子語類 [Collected Discourses by the Philosopher Ju (Shi)], the 1876 edition.

20. ———*Yilii Jingjuann Tongjiee* 儀禮經傳通解 (A General Survey of Ritual). Thirty-seven chapters (with a Supplement of Twenty-nine Chapters by Hwang Gann 黃榦). References are to the Japanese edition of 1662.

21. Jy An 芝庵 (Yuan period), *Jy An Chanq Luenn* 芝庵唱論 [Jy An's Discourse on Singing]. *Shin Cheu Yuann* 新曲苑 edition.

22. Lou Yueh 樓鑰, *Yueh Shu Jengwuh* 樂書正誤 [Corrections to the *Yueh Shu*], 1202. *Tzershyhjiu Tsorngshu* 擇是居叢書 edition.

23. Maa Duanlin 馬端臨 *Wenshiann Tongkao* 文獻通考 [*A Comprehensive Investigation of Documents and Traditions*]. 384 chapters, finished before 1319. Jehjiang Book Company edition of 1896.

24. Menq Yuanlao 孟元老, *Dongjing Menq Hwa Luh* 東京夢華録 [Recollections of the Splendor of the Eastern Capital], 1147. Ten chapters. Classics Press edition, Shanghai, 1956.

25. Nay Derueng 耐得翁, *Ducherng Jih Shenq* 都城紀勝 [The Wonders of the Capital], 1235. One chapter. Classics Press edition, Shanghai, 1956.

26. Nieh Chorngyih 聶崇義, *San Lii Twu* 三禮圖 [Illustrations for the Three Classics of Ritual], 996. Twenty chapters. *Syhbuh Tsorngkan* (3rd series) edition.

27. Roan Yih 阮逸 and Hwu Yuan 胡瑗, *Hwangyow Shin Yueh Twujih* 皇祐新樂圖記 [Illustrated Account of the Newly Revised Music of the Hwangyow Period], 1053, in three chapters. *Tsorngshu Jyicherng* edition.

28. Sheen Gua 沈括 (1031–1095), *Menqshi Biitarn* 夢溪筆談 [Memoirs at Menqshi]. Twenty-six chapters, first printed ca. 1086. Supplements: *Buu Biitarn* 補筆談 [Additional Memoirs], three chapters; *Shiuh Biitarn* 續筆談 [Further Memoirs], one chapter. All thirty chapters collated and annotated by Hwu Dawjinq 胡道静, *Menqshi Biitarn Jiawjenq* 夢溪筆談 校證, Shanghai, 1956.

29. Shyong Pernglai 熊朋來 (1246–1323), *Seh Puu* 瑟譜 [Treatise on the *Seh*]. *Tsorngshu Jyicherng* edition.

30. *Songq Hueyyaw* 宋會要 [A Compilation of State Regulations of Sonq]. Written during Sonq, restored in 1806 by Shyu Song 徐松, et al. Dahdong Book Company, 1936.

31. Taur Tzongyi 陶宗儀 (ca. 1330–1399), *Chuohgeng Cheu Luh* 輟耕曲録 [*Cheu Song* Notebook Written while at Rest from Farming]. *Shin Cheu Yuann* edition.

32. Tsay Yuandinq 蔡元定, *Liuhleu Shin Shu* 律呂新書 [A New Treatise on Regulating the Pitch Pipes], 1187. *Tsorngshu Jyicherng* edition.

33. Tuo Tuo 托托 and Ouyang Shyuan 歐陽玄, *Sonq Shyy* 宋史 [Sonq History—Standard History of the Sonq Dynasty], completed 1345. 496 chapters. Kaiming edition, 1934.

34. Wang Jihder 王驥德, *Cheu Liuh* 曲律 [Music of the *Cheu* Songs]. Preface dated 1610. *Jyy Hae* 指海 edition.

35. Wang Jwo 王灼 (died 1160), *Bihji Mannjyh* 碧鶏漫志 [Random Notes from Bihji]. *Tsyr Huah Tsorngbian* 詞話叢編 edition, 1935.

36. Wang Yinqlin 王應麟 (1223–1296), *Yuh Hae* 玉海 [Jade Sea Encyclopedia]. Two hundred chapters. Jehjiang Book Company edition, 1883.

37. Wu Tzyhmuh 呉自牧 (died 1275), *Menq Liang Luh* 夢梁録 [Recollections of a Dream Life (in Harngjou)]. Classics Press edition, 1956.

38. *Yueh Shu Yaw Luh* 樂書要録 [Essentials from Treatises on Music]. Anonymous, end of Seventh century; three chapters (fragmentary). Collated edition in *Tōyō Ongaku Kenkyū* 東洋音樂研究 (Journal of the Society for the Research of Asiatic Music); Tokyo, 1941, no. 3–4, ed. by Hazuka Keimei 羽塚啓明.

SECONDARY SOURCES

39. Aoki Masao 青木正兒, *Jonggwo Jinnshyh Shihcheu Shyy* 中國近世戲曲史 [History of Chinese Drama of the Recent Centuries]. Author's preface dated 1929. Translated into Chinese by Wang Guuluu 王古魯, 1931, and reprinted by the Writer's Press (作家出版社). Two volumes. Peking, 1958.

40. Bartlett-Wu, K. T., "Books on East Asiatic Music in the Library of Congress (Compiled before 1800): Works in Chinese." In the *Library of Congress Catalogue of Early Books on Music*. Supplement by Hazel Bartlett. Washington: Library of Congress, 1944, pp. 121–131.

41. Baxter, Glen William, *Index to the Imperial Register of Tz'u Prosody*. Harvard-Yenching Institute Studies, XV. Cambridge, Massachusetts, 1956.

42. ———"Metrical Origins of the Tz'u," *Harvard Journal of Asiatic Studies,* 16 (1953): 108–145.

43. Chao, Yuen Ren, "Tone, Intonation, Singsong, Chanting, Recitative. Tonal Composition and Atonal Composition in Chinese," in *For Roman Jakobson; Essays on the Occasion of His Sixtieth Birthday, 11 Oct., 1956.* Compiled by Morris Halle, et al. The Hague: Mouton and Co., 1956, pp. 52–59.

44. Chern Lii 陳澧, *Shengliuh Tongkao* 聲律通考 [A Historical Investigation of the Scale Systems]. Ten chapters. Canton, 1858.

45. Chiou Chyongsuen 丘琼蓀, *Bairshyr Dawren Gecheu Tongkao* 白石道人歌曲通考 [Comprehensive Investigation of the Songs by Whitestone the Taoist]. Peking: The Music Press, 音樂出版社 1959, 158 pp.

46. Chyan Wannchian 錢萬選, "Lihshimei Ling" 鬲溪梅令 [The Melody Lihshimei Ling], *Torngsheng Yuehkan* 同聲月刊, 2 (Nov. 1942): 1–4.

47. Courant, Maurice, "Essai historique sur la musique classique des chinois," in Lavignac and La Laurencie, *Encyclopédie de musique,* Paris, 1931, I, 77–241.

48. Day Charnggeng 戴長庚, *Liuh Huah* 律話 [Talks on Music], 1833.

49. Fang Cherngpei 方成培, *Shiangyanjiu Tsyr Juu* 香研居詞麈 [Chats on the Tsyr at the Fragrant Study Retreat]. Preface dated 1777. In *Dwushujai Tsorngshu* 讀書齋叢書, sec. II, fasc. 7–8.

50. Ferng Shoei 馮水, *Bairshyr Dawren Chyncheu "Guu Yuann" Shyh* 白石道人琴曲古怨釋 [Interpreting the *Chyn* Melody "Guu Yuann" by Whitestone the Taoist]. In *Ferng Shyh Yueh Shu* 馮氏樂書, vol. III (1924).

51. Gulik, R. H. van. *The Lore of the Chinese Lute.* Tokyo, 1940.

52. Hayashi Kenzō 林謙三 *Swei Tarng Yannyueh Diaw Yanjiou* 隋唐燕樂調研究 [Studies on the Modes of "Entertainment" Music in the Swei and Tarng Periods]. Translated into Chinese by Guo Mohruoh 郭沫若

Shanghai, 1936, 208 pp.

53. Hayashi Kenzō 林謙三 and Hirade Hisao 平出久永, "Biwa Kofu no Ken-kyū" 琵琶古譜の研究 (A Study of the Ancient Notation for the *P'i-pa*), *Gekkan Gakufu* 月刊樂譜 [Musical Monthly], Jan. 1938, pp. 23–58.

54. Hazuka Keimei 羽塚啓明, "Gakusho Yōroku Kaisetsu" 樂書要録解説 (Commentary on *Gaku-Sho-Yō-Roku*, a Musical book), *Tōyō Ongaku Kenkyū* 1940, no. 2.

55. Holzman, Donald, "Shen Kua and His Meng-Ch'i pi-t'an," *T'oung Pao*, vol. XLVI (1958), nos. 3–5, pp. 260–293.

56. Ja Fuhshi 查阜西 (compiler), *Shiann Tzay Guuchyn Cheu Chwanpuu Jieetyi Hueybian Chugao* 見在古琴曲傳譜解題彙編初稿. [Draft Compilation of the Names of all Existing *Chyn* Melodies in the Present Day with Bibliography of Sources and Annotation]. Four volumes. Limited, non-commercial edition published by the Institute of Ethnomusicology, Peking, 1956.

57. Jang Wenhuu 張文虎, *Shuyihshyh Yubii* 舒藝室餘筆 [Leftover Notes from the House of Leisurely Arts], 1862. In *Chyangtsuen Tsorngshu*, vol. XVIII.

58. Jenq Jenndwo 鄭振鐸, *Song Jin Yuan Jugongdiaw Kao* 宋金元諸宮調考 [A Study of the *Jugongdiaw* of the Sonq, Jin, and Yuan Periods]. First published in 1932; reprinted in his *Jonggwo Wenshyue Yanjiou* 中國文學研究 [Studies in Chinese Literature], Peking, 1957.

59. Jou Chinqyun 周慶雲, *Chyn Shu Tswenmuh* 琴書存目 [A Bibliography of *Chyn* Books]. Six chapters, 1914.

60. Ju Chianjy 朱謙之, "Ling Tyngkan *Yannyueh Kaoyuan Bar*" 凌廷堪燕樂考源跋 [A Colophon to Ling Tyngkan's Origin of Entertainment Music], appendix to the author's *Jonggwo Inyueh Wenshyue Shyy* 中國音樂文學史 [History of Chinese Musical Literature]. Shanghai: Commercial Press, 1935.

61. Kishibe Shigeo 岸邊成雄, "Tōdai ongaku bunken kaisetsu" 唐代音樂文獻解説 (A Short Bibliography on T'ang Music), *Tōyō Ongaku Kenkyū*, 1 (Nov. 1937): 69–73.

62. ———"Tō no zokugaku niju-hachi-chō no seiritsu nendai ni tsuite" 唐の俗樂二十八調の成立年代について (A Historical Study on the Twenty-eight Modes of the Popular Music in the T'ang Period), *Tōyō Gakuhō*, 26 (1939): 437–468 and 578–631; 27 (1939): 121–138.

63. Levis, John H. *Foundations of Chinese Musical Art*. Peiping, 1936. Reprinted by Paragon Book Reprint Corp. N. Y., 1963.

64. Lii Wenyuh 李文郁, "Dahshenq Fuu Kaoliueh" 大晟府考略 [Outline Study of the Dahshenq Institute], *Tsyrshyue Jihkan* 詞學季刊 [Quarterly of *Tsyr* Studies], Vol. II (1935), no. 2, pp. 7–32.

65. Lin Dahchuen 林大椿, *Tsyr Shyh* 詞式 [*Tsyr* Pattern Book]. Two vol-

umes. Shanghai: The Commercial Press, 1934.

66. Ling Jiingyan 凌景埏, "Sonq Wey Hannjing Yueh Yeu Dahshenq Fuu" 宋魏漢津樂與大晟府 (The Music of Wei Han-ching and the Ta-sheng Institute of the Sung Dynasty), *Yenching Journal of Chinese Studies,* 28 (Dec. 1940): 105–132.

67. Ling Tyngkan 凌廷堪, *Yannyueh Kaoyuan* 燕樂考源 [Origin of Entertainment Music], 1804. *Anhuei Tsorngshu* 安徽叢書, vol. IV.

68. *Mintzwu Inyueh Yanjiou Luennwenjyi* 民族音樂研究論文集 [Papers on Ethnomusicology], Peking: The Music Press. First Series, 1956; Second Series, 1957; Third Series, 1958.

69. Picken, Laurence, E. R. "Chiang K'uei's Nine Songs for Yueh," *Musical Quarterly,* 43 (1957): 201–219.

70. ———"China," *The New Oxford History of Music,* London and New York, 1957, I, 83–134.

71. ———"Secular Chinese Songs of the Twelfth Century," *Studia Musicologica Academiae Scientiarum Hungaricae,* 8 (1966), pp. 125–172.

72. ———"Twelve Ritual Melodies of the T'ang Dynasty," *Studia Memoriae Bela Bartok Sacra,* Aedes Academiae Scientiarum Hungariae, Budapest, 1956, pp. 147–173.

73. Sachs, Curt, *Rhythm and Tempo.* New York: Norton, 1953.

74. Sheen Shyong 沈雄, compiler, *Guu Jin Tsyr Huah* 古今詞話 [Past and Present Discourses on the *Tsyr*], 1689. Eight chapters. *Tsyr Huah Tsorngbian* 詞話叢編 edition.

75. Shiah Cherngtaur 夏承燾, *Bairshyr Dawren Gecheu Jiawliuh* 白石道人歌曲斠律 (The Editing of the Songs of Whitestone the Taoist), *The Yenching Journal of Chinese Studies,* 16 (1934): 83–117.

76. ———*Bairshyr Dawren Gecheu Parngpuu Biann* 白石道人歌曲傍譜辯 [Discussion on the Side Notation in the Songs of Whitestone the Taoist], *Yenching Journal of Chinese Studies,* 11 (1932): 2559–2588.

77. ———*Bairshyr Dawren Gecheu Parngpuu Biannjiaw Faa* 白石道人歌曲傍譜辯校法 [Methods of Collating the Side Notation in the Songs of Whitestone the Taoist], *Tsyr Shyue Jihkan* [Quarterly of *Tsyr* Studies], vol. I (1933), no. 3, pp. 17–31.

78. ———*Jiang Bairshyr Tsyr Bian nian Jianjiaw* 姜白石詞編年箋校 [A Chronological List of *Tsyr* by Jiang Bairshyr with Commentaries]. Shanghai: Jonghwa Book Company, 1958.

79. ———*Tarng Sonq Tsyr Luenntsorng* 唐宋詞論叢 [A Collection of Essays on the *Tsyr* of the Tarng and Sonq]. Shanghai, 1956.

80. ———*Tarng Sonq Tsyr-ren Nianpuu* 唐宋詞人年譜 [Biographies of *Tsyr* Poets of the Tarng and Sonq Dynasties]. Shanghai, 1955.

81. Shiah Jinqguan 夏敬觀, *Tsyrdiaw Suhyuan* 詞調溯源 (Tracing the Origins of *Tsyr* Tunes). Shanghai, 1931.

82. Taki Ryoichi 瀧遼一, "Ongaku shiryō no chōsa" 音樂資料の調査 [Report on the Investigation of Chinese Musical Source Materials,] *Tōhō Gakuhō* (Tokyo), 5 (1935): 215f.

83. Tarng Lan 唐蘭, "Bairshyr Dawren Gecheu Parngpuu Kao" 白石道人歌曲傍譜考 [A Study of the Side Notation in the Songs of Whitestone the Taoist], *Dongfang Tzarjyh*, 28 (1931): 65–74.

84. Torng Feei 童斐, *Jongyueh Shyunyuan* 中樂尋源 [The Origins of Chinese Music]. Shanghai: Commercial Press, 1936.

85. *Tsyr Yueh Tsorngkan* 詞樂叢刊 (A Symposium on the Ancient Musical Notations of *Tsyr*), by Rau Tzongyih 饒宗頤 and Jaw Tzongyuh 趙宗嶽. With a preface and a review by Yau Shinnong 姚莘農. Hong Kong: South Wind Publishing Company, 1958, 260 pp.

86. Uang Menqshu 汪孟舒, *Usylan Jyyfaa Shyh* 烏絲欄指法釋 [Annotations to the *Usylan* Manual]. Mimeographed edition, Peking, 1955.

87. Wang Guangchyi 王光祈, *Jonggwo Inyueh Shyy* 中國音樂史 [History of Chinese Music]. Two volumes. Shanghai: Jonghwa Book Company, 1934.

88. Wang Gwowei 王國維, *Sonq Yuan Shihcheu Shyy* 宋元戲曲史 (History of Sonq and Yuan Drama). Shanghai, 1915. Punctuated edition in Wang's collected works (王國維戲曲論文集) published by the Chinese Drama Press 中國戲曲出版社, Peking, 1957.

89. ———*Tarng Sonq Dahcheu Kao* 唐宋大曲考 (History of the Dance-suite of Tarng and Sonq). First edition, 1909; reprinted by the Chinese Drama Press, Peking, 1957.

90. Wang Jihlieh 王季烈, *Ynlu Cheu Tarn* 螾廬曲談 [Conversations on *Cheu* Songs at the Earthworm Hut]. Shanghai, 1928.

91. Wang Shyhshiang 王世襄, "Guuchyn Cheu Goanglingsann Shuoming" 古琴曲廣陵散說明 [On the *Chyn* Melody "Goanglingsann"], *Papers on Ethnomusicology*, second series, p. 25.

92. Yang Yinnliou 楊蔭劉, *Jonggwo Inyueh Shyygang* 中國音樂史綱 [Outline History of Chinese Music]. Postface dated Chungking, 1944. Shanghai: Wannyeh Book Company (萬葉書店), 1952, 342 pp.

93. ———"Koongmiaw Dingjih Inyueh de Chubuh Yanjiou" 孔廟丁祭音樂的初步研究 [A Preliminary Study of the Music of the Spring and Autumn Sacrificial Music in the Confucian Temple], *Inyueh Yanjiou* 音樂研究 (Journal of Music), vol. I (1958), no. 1, pp. 54–69.

94. ———*Sonq Jiang Bairshyr Chuanqtzuoh Gecheu Yanjiou* 宋姜白石創作歌曲研究 [Studies of the Songs Composed by Jiang Bairshyr of the Sonq Dynasty]. With annotation by In Fahluu 陰法魯. Institute of Ethnomusicology. Peking: The Music Press, 1957, 93 pp.

95. Yang Yinnliou 楊蔭劉 et al., compilers, *Jonggwo Inyueh Shyy Tsankao Twupiann* 中國音樂史參考圖片 [Photographic Illustrations of Musical

Materials for the Study of the History of Chinese Music]. Nine volumes to date. Published for the Institute of Ethnomusicology by the Music Press, Peking, 1955–.

Index

Academia Sinica, 24, 40n
Additional Memoirs, 30, 45, 59
Ambiguous symbols in popular notation, 58, 60
Ancient musical practices, 2
"Annshiang," 35, 99
Apel, Willi, 78n
Appoggiatura, 65, 125
Arpeggio on the *chyn*, 85
Art songs (*tsyr*), 72
Augmented fourth, 147
Auxiliary note, 65, 70

Bairshyr Dawren, *see* Jiang Kwei
Bairshyr puu, 59
Bann, 44
Banntzyh puu, 5
Banshehdiaw, 50, 54
Baoyantarng Mihjyi, 21n
Beat, 23, 73, 74, 93
"Beengong Poh Tzyy," 28, 129
Bei-in, 231
Bells: number in a set, 1, 5, 14; illustrations of, 2; measurements of, 3; pitches of, 18, 31; ancient specimens of, 31; performance on, 93
Bian-chinq, 93n
Bian-jong, 93n
Biann in Tsay Yuandinq's tone system, 8n, 93n
Biann tones, 5, 8n, 19
Bibliographies, 1n, 7, 16–19 *passim*, 29n
Bih, 91
Bih-cheu, 8, 57n
Biographies, 15, 19
Biwa, 58n
Boh, 82
Boh-jong, 93n
Book of Songs, see *Classic of Poetry*
"Bor Jiu," 188
Borrowing of melodic phrases, *see* Melody, types and relations
Budonq, 87
Buu Biitarn, 30, 51

Cadence, 21, 27, 31, 43–45, 50, 67; on the higher octave, 10n, 155; irregular, 33, 55, 56, 57n, 70, *see also*

Fann; irregular in *chyn* music, 146; secondary, 61–66, 128; final, 61, 65, 66, 71
Caesura in *tsyr*, 100
Cambiata, 65, 70n, 125
Ceremonial music, 4, 5, 9, 18, 19, 42; of Southern Sonq, 7; ritual songs, 9–11, 36; Ritual Songs for Yueh, 34, 37, 70, 174; performance of, 93, 94–96
Chanting poetry, 72, 96
"Charngtyngyuann Mann," 35, 99
Charnlinq, 74
Chaur Shyh Jyh, 17n
Cheh, 60, 67, 69, 96n, 97
Chern Jihru, 21n
Chern Jiushyh, 81n
Chern Jwo, 81n
Chern Lii, 9
Chern Shyh, 81n, 82–89 *passim*
Chern Yang, 4, 15, 45n, 89
Chern Yuanjinq, 23
Cherng Shyong, 85
Cherng Yuh, 89
Cherng Yuhjiann, 29n
"Chernggwo Gong Tzeng Tzyy," 189
Cherngsheng, 86
Cheu, 38, 39, 58n
Cheu Liuh, 28n, 67, 68
Cheujong, 91
"Chi Yueh," 188
Chianchiing Tarng Shumuh, 41
Chii-diaw, 8
"Chiliang Fann," 35, 99
Chimes, 2, 3, 5, 14, 31, 93
Ching: as prefix, 44, 155, 190; as suffix, 93
"Ching Miaw," 189
Chingshangdiaw, 80
Chiou Chyongsuen, 68n, 72n, Chap. IV *passim*
Chiou Jyluh, 96, 155
"Chioushiau Yn," 35, 99
Chiufuh, 96n
Chorngshyng, 74, 76
Chorngtour, 74–76
Chorngwen Tzoongmuh, 17
Chou pyiba, 5n
Chuoh, 86

INDEX

INDEX

INDEX

INDEX

INDEX